The Troubadours

Covering one of the most fascinating yet misunderstood periods in history, the MEDIEVAL LIVES series presents medieval people, concepts and events, drawing on political and social history, philosophy, material culture (art, architecture and archaeology) and the history of science. These books are global and wide-ranging in scope, encompassing both Western and non-Western subjects, and span the fifth to the fifteenth centuries, tracing significant developments from the collapse of the Roman Empire onwards.

SERIES EDITOR: Deirdre Jackson

Albertus Magnus and the World of Nature *Irven M. Resnick and Kenneth F. Kitchell Jr*

Alle Thyng Hath Tyme: Time and Medieval Life *Gillian Adler and Paul Strohm*

Andrey Rublev: The Artist and His World *Robin Milner-Gulland*

The Art of Anatomy in Medieval Europe *Taylor McCall*

The Art of Medieval Falconry *Yannis Hadjinicolaou*

Bede and the Theory of Everything *Michelle P. Brown*

Christine de Pizan: Life, Work, Legacy *Charlotte Cooper-Davis*

Francis of Assisi: His Life, Vision and Companions *Michael F. Cusato*

Geoffrey Chaucer: Unveiling the Merry Bard *Mary Flannery*

Marco Polo and His World *Sharon Kinoshita*

Margery Kempe: A Mixed Life *Anthony Bale*

The Teutonic Knights: Rise and Fall of a Religious Corporation *Aleksander Pluskowski*

The Troubadours *Linda M. Paterson*

THE TROUBADOURS

LINDA M. PATERSON

REAKTION BOOKS

In memory of Simon Gaunt, friend and wise counsellor
Quals perd'e quals dans es!

Published by Reaktion Books Ltd
Unit 32, Waterside
44–48 Wharf Road
London N1 7UX, UK

www.reaktionbooks.co.uk

First published 2024

Printed and bound in India by Replika Press Pvt. Ltd

A catalogue record for this book is available from the British Library

ISBN 978 1 78914 919 7

CONTENTS

Preface

This book is designed to be accessible to anyone interested in or curious about the medieval troubadours. Quotations are mainly in English translation, aiming to convey both the sense and some of the spirit and rhythm of the original Occitan, though the original is sometimes quoted in order to highlight the form and sounds of the poetry. Musical performances are widely available on YouTube as well as CDs; the Introduction reflects on different approaches to modern musical interpretations.

Historical figures other than troubadours are normally referred to here by commonly recognized anglicized forms, such as Richard the Lionheart, Eleanor of Aquitaine and William X of Aquitaine, though less well-known figures, such as Ramón Berenguer of Barcelona, retain their local forms. The first troubadour's role as historical figure and troubadour intertwines and 'Guilhem IX' is used for both. Folquet de Marselha is first active as a troubadour, but after he renounces this role to become a bishop, I refer to him as Fulk of Toulouse.

Jongleurs, miniature from *Tropaire-Prosaire à l'usage d'Auch*, 990–1010.

Introduction

The troubadours were poet-musicians composing in Occitan, the language of what is now the south of France, as opposed to the Old French language of the northern French *trouvères*. Some were women. We know of 460 named troubadours through various sources: the thirteenth- and fourteenth-century manuscripts that have preserved their songs; contemporary documents, such as witness lists; information provided by the songs themselves; and references to them by other medieval writers. More than 2,500 pieces have survived. If authors composed for oral performance to particular audiences at specific times and places, their contemporaries and successors did not see their lyrics as ephemeral occasional pieces. They preserved them through a long process of oral and written transmission. Texts surviving in a single manuscript or loose-leaf folio, or cited within a narrative text, suggest the disappearance of many more that do not conform to a mainstream literary canon.

It is convenient to distinguish troubadours as composers from jongleurs or performers, even if some individuals could be both at the same time or move from one activity to the other, and even if the medieval terminology is more complicated than this.[1] Arnaut Daniel, the troubadour most highly praised by Dante, is said to have been a gentleman who learned *letras* (letters) well and delighted in *trobar* (composing), then 'abandoned letters and made himself into a jongleur, and took on a manner of composing in difficult rhymes, so that his songs are not easy either to understand or to learn by heart'.[2] Here the act of becoming a jongleur does not mean he gave up composing – quite the contrary – but rather that he made a living as an itinerant performer.

Some troubadours had their own jongleurs: Guiraut de Borneil apparently had two that he took with him to perform

Jongleurs, miniature from *Cancioneiro da Ajuda*, 13th century.

Guiraut de Borneil with two jongleurs, historiated initial from a *Chansonnier provençal* manuscript, 13th century.

his songs during his summer tours of the courts.[3] A troubadour might sometimes send a jongleur with a song as a message: at the time of the Third Crusade, Bertran de Born dispatched his jongleur Papiol to Tyre via the Savoie and Brindisi to tell Conrad he intended to join him.[4] Each itinerant jongleur had his own repertoire of lyrics, and would sometimes ask a troubadour to give him a song. This would not only enlarge the jongleur's professional baggage but could give the troubadour an opportunity to compose a comical piece insulting him for his ugly, shabby appearance and questionable habits.[5]

Historical and cultural environment

'Occitania' (pronounced 'Oxitania') is a convenient word for designating the lands of the troubadours' origins, but it never existed as a political entity. The main contenders for power until the early thirteenth century were the dukes of Aquitaine, the

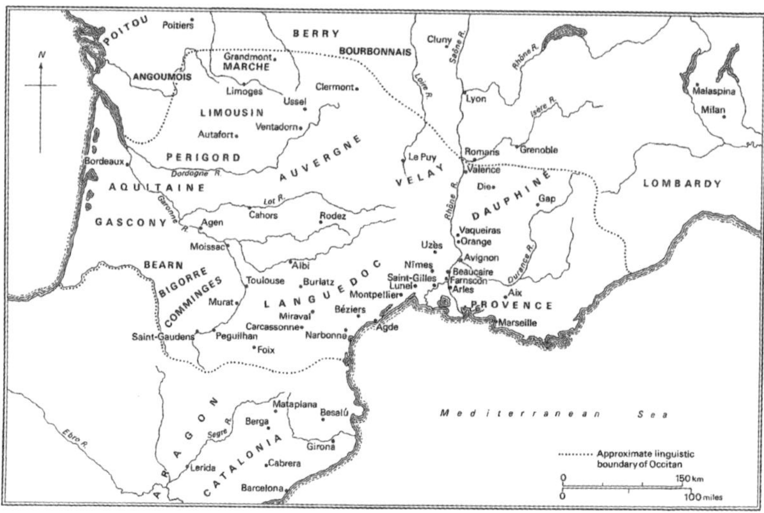

Map of Occitania and neighbouring Catalonia, 12th–13th centuries.

counts of Toulouse and the kings of Aragon-Catalonia. When William IX came to power in 1086, the dukes of Aquitaine effectively controlled a greater part of present-day France. Poitou and Aquitaine passed to the Plantagenets after Eleanor of Aquitaine's marriage to the future Henry II of England in 1152 and his accession to the throne in 1154. The Languedoc, from Toulouse to the Rhône, was dominated by the counts of Toulouse. Aragon and Catalonia, united in 1137 under Ramón Berenguer IV, held Roussillon and enclaves in the upper Languedoc; its count-kings struggled with the counts of Toulouse throughout the twelfth century for control of Provence with a view to creating a Mediterranean state from the Garonne and Ebro to the Alps. Occitania also contained many other independent or semi-autonomous areas, such as the Pyrenean baronies of Béarn, Bigorre, Comminges and Foix, or the Auvergne, in theory directly dependent on the duchy of Aquitaine rather than the French crown. Many cities fell outside the dominance of the main territorial lords. Albi, Carcassonne, Béziers, Agde and Nîmes were controlled by the powerful Trencavels; Narbonne and Montpellier had their own independent rulers; Marseille remained independent of Provence until 1252, while Toulouse was by the end of the twelfth century well on its way to becoming an independent republic.[6]

Occitan identity is embodied not in its political boundaries but its language and culture. Its language was the language of *oc*, its word for 'yes', as opposed to *oïl* (French) or *sí* (Italian), and known as *lengua romana* as opposed to Latin. The troubadours' language is a literary koiné or common language that effaces or blurs differences of dialect.[7] These composer-performers and their culture spread far beyond the linguistic boundaries of Occitan. Troubadours travelled abroad in search of patronage, especially to northern Spain and Italy, but also to Hungary and courts in Thessalonica and Tripoli in the Holy Land. As part of his strategy of furthering his political ambitions in Provence, the king, Alfonso II of Aragon, adopted their language as his court's official literary language.[8] Troubadour culture also exercised powerful influence on the *trouvères* of northern France, the German *Minnesänger* and the Galego-Portuguese poets.

Occitan courtly lyrics first appeared at the end of the eleventh century with the earliest known troubadour, Duke Guilhem IX of Aquitaine, just as the vernacular *chanson de geste* was emerging in the north with the *Chanson de Roland*. Until after the mid-twelfth century these lyrics were restricted to a small number of courts and composers, including some outstanding figures such as Jaufre Rudel, Marcabru, Peire d'Alvernhe and Bernart Marti. During the second half of the twelfth century, the so-called golden age of troubadour song, these lyrics flourished through the brilliance of some extraordinarily talented poet-musicians: Bernart de Ventadorn, Raimbaut d'Aurenga, Bertran de Born, Arnaut Daniel, Peire Vidal, Guiraut de Borneil, Gaucelm Faidit, Raimbaut de Vaqueiras and more. This development took place amid the explosion of philosophical and

Alfonso II of Aragon, folio from *Liber feudorum maior*, late 12th century.

German *Minnesänger* and courtly love, folio from the *Codex Manesse*, c. 1300–1340.

scientific ideas, Romanesque art and architecture, historiography, law, travel and trade, known as the twelfth-century Renaissance, when vernacular literature began to blossom all over Europe. While courtly ideas from the troubadours penetrated the north during the second half of the century, this period coincided with the rise of chivalry in northern France: idealistic concepts of what it meant to be a knight, expressed especially in the new French chivalric romance. Many troubadours were knights, but Occitan culture at this time was courtly, not chivalric. Any beginnings of assimilating knightly violence to courtly or religious ideals, in imitation of northern models, may well have been stymied by southern experience of French militarism during the Albigensian Crusade: the invasion of the Languedoc by the troops of Simon de Montfort under the auspices of the Church, which sought to extirpate the Cathar heresy. Its consequences included the dispersal of many troubadours to north Italy and the Iberian peninsula in search of patronage, and a flourishing literature of revolt and resistance in the form of political and polemical songs.

The troubadours' social circumstances

The thirteenth- and fourteenth-century manuscripts transmitting the surviving troubadour songs date from at least a century and a half after the death of Guilhem IX. They are nevertheless an important source of information about the troubadours' lives and social condition. Like their modern counterparts, consumers of the songbooks were curious about the songs' authors: their lives, social background and the circumstances giving rise to the poems. This led some compilers to preface a song or group of songs with a potted biography called a *vida* or 'Life', and/or a *razo*, a more or less hypothetical account of the political or amorous situation behind a certain piece or group of pieces, frequently extrapolated from the texts themselves. There are about one hundred *vidas*, covering under a quarter of the 460 troubadours whose names have survived, and nearly all say something about a troubadour's social background. The majority of these biographies were brought to Italy by the troubadour Uc de St Circ, who, after travelling extensively through the courts of the Midi and north Italy, ended up in Treviso at the court of Ezzelino and Alberico da Romano in around 1220. While the evidence of the *vidas* cannot be assumed to be reliable without corroboration, especially given the passage of time, it is not unreasonable to suppose that Uc was able to gather a lot of information from the people he met during his travels. Much of it has been authenticated or amplified by other sources, particularly archival material, available in the *Dizionario biografico dei Trovatori*.[9]

The table over the page sets out figures for troubadours of different social conditions identified in these various sources. Since the *Dizionario* includes all cases found in the *vidas*, the *Dizionario*'s figures here give additional examples. Queries and hyphenated figures indicate cases deemed probable or doubtful. Social categories were not always defined by clear boundaries, and belonging to a noble family might not indicate a position of any power or wealth; in the upper nobility, titles such as 'king', 'count', 'viscount' and so on are clear enough, but less clear are the epithets 'lord' or 'gentleman'. Knights can be poor, but a prestigious consul can also be described as a knight or from a knightly family. A king or a count will also be a knight, but this is taken for granted in the sources and is not specified. Nobles in the table include both titled persons and family members.

The figures are revealing. They show a considerable range of conditions, but also a vast preponderance of troubadours from aristocratic and knightly families. While many of the upper nobility have left us few pieces, from the highest levels of society nobles clearly regarded engaging in *trobar* as a badge of cultural

Social status of troubadours

	Vidas	*Dizionario*	*Total*
UPPER NOBILITY	35–6	62–71	97–107
king	1	3	4
duke	1 (also a count)		1
count	4–5	7	11–12
marquis	1		1
prince	2		2
viscount	3	8	11
comtor		1	1
baron or 'bars'	6	4	10
castellan	15	1	16
gentleman, lord	2	38–47	40–49
KNIGHTS	24	14–15	38–9
urban knight		5	5
poor knight	7		7
son of poor knight	5		5
son of poor vavassor	1		1
minor knight		1–2	1–2
unspecified	11	8	19
BURGHERS	10–11	19–24	29–35
consul or high officer		5–7	5–7
merchant		4	4
merchant's son	3–4		3–4
artisan	2		2
Jew		1	1
banker		1	1
unspecified	1	8–11	9–12
burgher family	4		4
JUDICIARY	1	5–6	6–7
judge	1	3	4
legal expert		2–3	2–3

	Vidas	*Dizionario*	*Total*
CLERGY	10	17–20	27–30
bishop		2	2
provost		1	1
canon	4	2?	4–6?
abbot		1?	1?
prior		1	1
monk	2	1	3
friar		2	2
in military order		4	4
teacher	1	3	4
scribe		2[10]	2
unspecified cleric	3	1	4
DOCTORS		1?	1?
JONGLEURS	14	19–33	33–46

status. King Alfonso II of Aragon famously debated with Guiraut de Borneil as to whether a powerful nobleman could ever be a true courtly lover;[11] his descendant Peter III, at a time of crisis when the army of Philip III of France was invading his territory, chose to contribute, in the troubadours' Occitan tongue, to songs of poetic propaganda exchanged across the Pyrenees.[12] Counts, viscounts and their relatives across the Midi, north Italy and Catalonia, some of whom were female, such as Maria de Ventadorn, were both poets and patrons. Castellans might be rich or much less so: Austorc del Boy's family owned various castles, whereas Raimon de Miraval, described in his *vida* as a poor knight, had to share his with three other family members, the result of common practices dividing property equally among male heirs in parts of the south of modern-day France.[13] Equally if not more variable in power and status were men designated indeterminately in the *vidas* as baron or *bar*, including Savaric de Malleo, a seneschal to John of England, and Guiraut de Cabrera, from one of the greatest feudal families of Catalonia, in contrast to Blacatz and his son Blacasset, Provençal noblemen of tenuously slender means. The extensive category of 'gentlemen' or 'lords' also covers a breadth of wealth and status. Only two of these come from the *vidas*, but the *Dizionario* pinpoints a great many more, including women such as Clara d'Anduza, Iseut de Capion and Isabella. The preponderance of knightly families among troubadours and their audiences accounts for the troubadours' recourse in their love songs to the feudal vocabulary of fidelity oaths, homage and loyal service – even if it strays into the less aristocratic language of serfdom.[14]

Knightly troubadours and their relatives tended to be poor by comparison with the upper nobility, except for urban knights who might enjoy considerable wealth and local power. Knights of noble birth lived in all Occitan towns, as they did in Spain and Italy, unlike in northern France, where the nobility almost always lived in the countryside. Knights in towns such as Arles, Nîmes and Carcassonne,

Bonifaci Calvo, historiated initial from a *Chansonnier provençal* manuscript, 13th century.

Monk of Montaudon, historiated initial from a *Chansonnier provençal* manuscript, 13th century.

> thought to be descendants of men in whom ecclesiastical or lay lords had entrusted city defence, transformed the remains of Roman theatres, arenas, gateways and temples into a collection of fortresses . . . These city knights gradually took over rights to control trade in such important commodities as salt and wool, and by the twelfth century had become the dominant element in numerous major cities.[15]

The borderline between urban knights and powerful burghers is fluid. Burgher troubadours can be found among such prestigious figures as the consuls Guilhem Fabre or Olivier de la Marche, members of city oligarchies that included these and other high officials such as judges and legal experts. Lanfranc Cigala was a judge and knight in Genoa. Merchants such as the oil producer Joan Esteve de Beziers and the banker Bonifaci Calvo were troubadours, and some of the best-known were merchants' sons: Folquet de Marselha, who became a bishop; Aimeric de Peguilhan, son of a cloth merchant; and perhaps Peire Vidal, said to be a furrier's son.[16] Guillem Figueira was a tailor, Elias Cairel a gold- and

Perdigon with fiddle, historiated initial from *Recueil des poésies des troubadours*, 13th century.

silversmith who designed armour.[17] Clergy too could be troubadours. They included two bishops, a provost, several canons, a prior and possibly an abbot, monks and friars, scribes and simple clerics, teachers such as Guiraut de Borneil, and members of military orders. The surgeon Raimon of Avignon may be the troubadour of that name.

While jongleurs were essentially performers, they might also compose songs. Pistoleta worked as a singer for a troubadour but then became one himself and 'composed *cansos* with attractive tunes'.[18] The *vidas* reveal how knowledge of letters and the art of composing attractive words and music was a strong factor in social mobility.[19] According to his *vida*, Perdigon was the son of a poor fisherman who through his intelligence and *trobar* rose to great esteem and honour, Dalfi d'Alvernhe regarding him as his knight and giving him clothes and arms, land and income.

As with other social groups, the condition of jongleurs was variable. On the one hand, Guilhem Magret and Uc de Pena were described as lowlife gamblers and frequenters of taverns; on the other, Peire Salvatge became the king's jongleur, rewarded by Peter III with a salary, while the Italian Ferrari de Ferrara, a 'master jongleur' at the house of Este, was regarded by the marquises of Este as a champion and authority on the art of *trobar*, ready to answer any questions on it to anyone who understood the 'Provençal tongue'.[20]

The courts

For troubadours who were not rich enough to live by independent means, courts provided the main source of patronage. A court is essentially an assembly centred on the person of a lord: in other words it is where the lord – or his wife – is. It could evoke not only a place but a series of places, since courts could be mobile, especially in the case of great princes, obliged to travel throughout their lands for the purposes of government and administration.[21] Occasionally a great court festival, such as the wedding of Eleanor of England to Alfonso VIII of Castile in 1170,[22] would see troubadours and jongleurs flocking from hundreds of miles around in the hope of generous rewards. Seigneurial courts were a more intimate affair, from the troubadour's point of view ideally offering domestic comforts, male and female company, cultured conversation, courteous attention without aloofness from the aristocracy, and gifts. For Raimbaut de Vaqueiras, this ideal was embodied in the court of his patron Boniface of Montferrat: 'In your court reign all graces: the giving of gifts and the courting of ladies, fine clothes, elegant armour, trumpets, games, viols and song; and you never liked to have a doorkeeper at mealtimes.' Folquet de Lunel claimed that this ideal prevailed at the court of Alfonso X of Castile:

> He holds a court where no gentleman can wait in vain
> for his gift, a court without extortion or violence, a court

Alfonso x of Castile with musicians and scribe, miniature from *Cantigas de Santa María – Códice de los músicos*, 13th century.

> where people listen to reason: a court without pride
> and a court without baseness, a court where there are
> a hundred donors who often make unsolicited gifts,
> as rich as solicited ones, from certain kings I know.

It is not hard to read between the lines and see how this ideal was not always reality, and elsewhere troubadours complain of the avarice of lords who starve their household and hob-nob with flatterers and backbiters.[23]

While many composers did indeed travel the courts, their hope was to find some more permanent employment. Until the death of his patron William x of Aquitaine Marcabru seems to have enjoyed a steady position in Poitiers, though it is unlikely that he or any other troubadour made his living by *trobar* alone: Cercamon had clerical training and the possibility of employment from the clergy, and Marcabru was an educated man with an ecclesiastical bias, and was possibly retained as some kind of household clerk.[24] Raimbaut de Vaqueiras spent some years moving from one court to another before being taken on permanently by Boniface of Montferrat, who, exceptionally, knighted him: we know that Raimbaut served in his army as well as being his companion in youthful exploits.[25] Bertran d'Alamanon was a landowner employed by the Count of Anjou in a bureaucratic capacity, so was very unlikely to have relied on his poetry for his main income.

It might be assumed that the lower down the social scale the poet-musician was, the more dependent he was likely to be on patronage. Many troubadours did, clearly, voice the views of their actual or potential patrons and celebrate their qualities and achievements; but they could sometimes be very free in their expression. Bertran d'Alamanon told Charles of Anjou in diplomatic but no uncertain terms not to waste time on Louis IX's first crusade; Sordel wrote scurrilously about his alleged sexual proclivities.[26]

Poetic genres

Troubadours composed in a variety of poetic genres, from love songs to satirical and polemical pieces, laments for the dead (*planhs*), dialogue songs, burlesque and obscene pieces and crusading exhortations. In the early days nearly all their songs were usually called *vers*, but by the second half of the twelfth century a love song was known as a *canso*. This was the most highly regarded lyric genre, where words and tune were almost always original creations. Other genres were usually modelled on a *canso*, borrowing in whole or in part its tune and formal structure: the number and syllabic length of its lines, its rhyme scheme and rhyme endings. The *sirventes* treated political, military, moralizing or other non-amorous topics. Dialogue songs included the *partimen*, where one singer chose a topic for debate and which side to defend, thus constraining his or her opponent to defend the opposite side, and the *tenso*, which left the second singer free to choose their own point of view.[27] Many songs included references to crusading, exhorting men to go on crusade, describing their experiences or sorrow at leaving a loved one behind, or blaming tardy leaders, though it is hard to define a specific genre of 'crusade song': such elements are often mixed in with other themes, and indeed generic boundaries as a whole are fluid and tend to be imposed by later theorists, either medieval or modern. Many of Guiraut de Borneil's songs, for example, mix amorous and moralizing themes. The troubadour corpus also includes a number of burlesque songs of considerable obscenity, often accompanied by extremely dextrous rhyming and wordplay that may be linked to a centuries-old jongleuresque tradition.[28]

Poetic craft

It would be hard to overestimate the extent to which troubadours and their audiences valued the complexity and variety of their compositional craft, in whatever genre. The surviving troubadour songs involve nearly nine hundred different metrical structures,[29] and it is hard to know how our poet-musicians kept track of others' creations as they sought to shape a new and original form. To gain a glimpse of the dazzling variety of ways in which they interlaced words and rhymes, quite apart from musical elements, one has only to look at Dominique Billy's book on the architecture of medieval Occitan and Old French lyrics.[30]

The troubadours also developed a range of different poetic styles, such as *trobar clus*, a 'closed' style involving layers of meaning or difficulty of comprehension; *trobar leu*, a 'light' and accessible style; *trobar ric* or *car*, which sought out rare words and rhymes; *trobar plan* or a smooth style; *trobar prim*, involving tightly chiselled sounds and images; and *trobar brau*, which exploited harsh, rough sounds and was particularly (though not exclusively) suited to poetry of invective.[31]

Music

Music is integral to troubadour poetry, as the troubadours say themselves. Of his famous crusade song *Pax in nomine Domini* Marcabru announces that he 'made the words and the tune'; Bernart Marti declares that the troubadour's art consists in making 'new, fresh tunes' and 'lacing and binding up beautiful words'; Bertran Carbonel describes the reciprocal roles of text and tune through the simile of a mill, where the verbal composition needs music to make it function productively: 'A *cobla* [single-stanza piece] without a melody is like a mill without water; anyone who composes a *cobla* is wrong not to give it one, for one has no joy of the mill but from what it produces.'[32] Looking back at the troubadour tradition in the early fourteenth century, Dante also testifies to the dual nature of the troubadour *canso*, as a poetic genre that is sung and at the same time as a carefully preserved written text.[33]

Some of the thirteenth- and fourteenth-century medieval songbooks also make this clear, containing musical notation for some texts, and empty staves for some others showing an original intention to include tunes for the songs to which they are attached. Melodies for about 250 troubadour songs survive: a tenth of the total lyric corpus. While the northern French lyric tradition transmits over ten times as many tunes, such disparity is unlikely to have arisen from a lack of interest in troubadour music on the compilers' part, since the empty staves indicate that they were hoping to be able to provide notation for more tunes than they had to hand. Francesco Carapezza explains the disparity by the greater genealogical and geographical compactness of the French tradition, observing that the troubadour manuscripts were put together in different places under diverse conditions of production and in individual copying workshops that, for various reasons, did not plan for the collaboration of a specialist such as

Song of Guiraut Riquier, from a *Chansonnier provençal* manuscript, 14th century.

a musical scribe. In addition, the Occitan lyrics contained a high incidence of poetic genres for which an original (as opposed to a borrowed) tune was not an essential element, such as satirical and topical poetry and dialogue poems, as well as so-called non-lyric genres.[34]

However, the many comments about musical ability show that for the songbooks' public, this was still a key component of the troubadours' art. So, for example, Arnaut de Maroill 'was good at composing (*trobar*)' and 'sang well', and Pons de Capdoill 'was good at *trobar* and playing the vielle and singing'.[35] One (probably apocryphal) *razo* gives an idea of how the composition process might have gone. It describes how an unknown jongleur at Richard the Lionheart's court challenged Arnaut Daniel, known for his difficult rhymes, to a poetry competition, claiming he could outdo him. Each composer gave his palfrey as a pledge to the king, who shut them away in a room, giving them a ten-day deadline. Arnaut, fed up, proved unable to lace one word with another, while the unknown jongleur composed his piece quickly and easily. After five days the jongleur asked him if he had finished, and Arnaut lied that he had done so three days ago. While the jongleur spent his nights practising his song out loud in order to remember it properly, Arnaut listened to it and learned it by heart. Brought before the king, Arnaut asked to go first and proceeded to sing the jongleur's song. When the truth came out the king found it a huge joke and rewarded both of them.[36]

How did troubadour music relate to earlier song in Latin and the vernacular? As the professor of music and medieval studies John Haines has shown, 'most of the evidence for song in early Romance languages survives from the third century onwards in the form of condemnations.' These imply the widespread practice of folk music, in particular women's songs such as funeral laments and ring dances, with some cases showing the influence of lay or pre-Christian music on medieval devotional song.[37] The presence of three religious songs in Occitan, or Occitan and Latin, among Latin songs called *versus* in the oldest part of a manuscript of St Martial of Limoges, datable to around 1100, has suggested links between such Latin songs and *vers*, the term used for songs by early troubadours. Carapezza has described how the sporadic presence of stanzaic types in this codex, similar to those favoured by Guilhem IX and written during his lifetime in the environment of an abbey that enjoyed relations with the dukes of Aquitaine, has traditionally been taken as proof of Guilhem's adoption of paraliturgical formal (and musical) models, but he argues that there may have already existed more complex connections between the *nova cantica* of the Aquitanian school and an unattested profane lyric tradition.[38] In his view, the strongest argument suggesting the existence of a contemporary and even previous lyric tradition before Guilhem is that of the stylistic and formal elaboration of his poetry, which shows a high standard of literariness and tends to define a courtly cultural system, including the selectivity of listeners.[39]

The songbooks only appear some two centuries after the original composition of troubadour tunes. These we cannot access. As Margaret Switten pithily puts it, 'no medieval sounds have come down to us.'[40] The records we do have suffer from not only the time lag but from variations (some tunes are found in more than one manuscript), changes in systems of notation and the role of memory and multiple performances in the transmission of songs produced for oral rendition. Words and music were transmitted differently. Songbook compilers had access to written sources, now almost entirely lost: copies of songs in previous collections, single parchment sheets, occasionally a complete book devoted to a single poet. But Anna Radaelli's research has shown that the tunes that have survived must for the most part have had a very restricted circulation, so the collectors will have had considerable difficulty in finding exemplars furnished with musical notation from which they could copy the tunes, or even someone who knew the tunes.

All this does not necessarily mean that over this period the tunes changed out of all recognition. What happened to them in the meantime? Songs continued to circulate orally in the repertoire of jongleurs, and the versification and words provided some element of stability. In addition they were often reused in *contrafacta*: songs which borrowed the versification of models, usually prestigious *cansos*, and by implication their melodies. Such reuse could demonstrably span a considerable length of time: in the late thirteenth century Guiraut Riquier modelled several songs on a famous piece by Raimbaut de Vaqueiras composed in 1201; songs by Guilhem de Cabestanh and Gui d'Ussel, composed around 1200, were known and sung by Giovanni da Cascia, the earliest composer of Italian *ars nova*, who was active in the great courts of Lombardy and the Veneto during the first half of the fourteenth century.[41] Songs could indeed have a long life in oral transmission. Particularly interesting is the so-called *Jeu de sainte Agnès*, an early fourteenth-century religious drama from the Hérault containing lyric insertions accompanied by musical notation based on pre-existing songs, both religious and profane. The insertions are indicated in the manuscript by the formula *in sonu* ('to the tune of'), followed by the incipit of the musical model written above the first stanza of the *contrafactum*. One of these is an adaptation of the tune of Guiraut de Borneil's well-known dawn-song *Reis glorios*. Another is a fragment of a tune attributed to Guilhem IX, identified on the basis of the metre and the content of the *contrafactum* as *Pos de chantar m'es pres talens*, for which no other notation has survived.[42] From his analysis of the musical notation in the *Jeu de sainte* Agnès Carapezza is able to conclude that, while it would not be legitimate to reconstruct with any precision the music of William's *vers* on the basis of the slight fragment, substantial similarity could still be reasonably postulated between them.[43]

The Italian musicologist's analyses show that surviving tunes generally adhere in type to the genre of the text, as advised in thirteenth- and fourteenth-century poetic and musical treatises. The latest version of Guilhem Molinier's *Leys d'Amors* (1328–37) prescribes for the *vers* and *canso* 'slow, solemn and new music, with beautiful, melodious rises and falls, with beautiful passages (ornaments?) and pleasing pauses, while the *pastorela* always requires a new tune, pleasing and lively, not slow like that of the *vers* or *canso*, but a little more flowing and quick', and the *dansa* 'should have a joyful and lively tune for dancing, but not as slow as a *vers* or *canso*, but a little quicker for dancing'.[44] While it is hard to decide whether such generic differentiation is always due to the author of the text or to some anonymous musical composer, Marcabru's surviving melodies certainly fulfil these requirements. The treatises assimilate the *planh* (funeral lament) to the *vers* and *canso* in terms of the difficulty of the musical composition, which in this case should be 'as if lamenting', and Gaucelm Faidit's famous *planh* on the death of Richard the Lionheart assuredly conforms to this in the use of the lower part of the range and the 'calculated distribution of neumatic and syllabic transitions, lending it a melancholic and solemn pace'.[45]

Carapezza also demonstrates that if the love song or *canso*, which evolves from the early *vers*, is presented as the musically dominant genre in the manuscript tradition and early treatises, this does not mean it is homogeneous in style and form from one end of the troubadour tradition to the other. The genre develops musically as well as textually. The typically seven- or eight-syllable love song of Bernart de Ventadorn is not the same as the late twelfth-century *cansos* of great troubadours such as Gaucelm Faidit, Folquet de Marselha and Peire Vidal, who choose predominantly decasyllabic stanzaic structures, or the work of the late thirteenth-century troubadour Guiraut Riquier, who favours elaborate ornamentation. Just as many composers experiment with textual form and content, so do many – but not necessarily the same ones – experiment with the music. The success of some conventional troubadours such as Peirol and Raimon de Miraval may be down to the quality of the music of their songs.[46]

While a *canso* was usually expected to have an original tune, the complete or partial reuse of tunes and versification was widespread in other genres, particularly the *sirventes*. Sometimes this is explicit: Bertran de Born, for example, declares he wants to give Richard the Lionheart 'advice to the tune of Lady Alamanda'. Several such cases refer to the tunes drawn from non-lyric genres: epics, from which come the melodies of (Peire de) Mont Rabei, Boves d'Antona and Gui (de Nanteuil); perhaps liturgical genres, such as Marcabru's *Lo vers comensa/ e son so vieill antic*; and very probably folkloric ones (Guilhem de Berguedà, imitating the *chantaret* or 'little song' of the children of Pau).[47] If there are not more such mentions, Carapezza argues, this was because there was no need to cite tunes taken from famous songs: the audience would simply recognize them. However, as he observes, they give us a glimpse of the troubadours' musical culture, which appears from the start as varied and complex, certainly not confined to Latin and monastic origins but open to influences from other levels of culture and traditions of adjacent vernacular songs now submerged.

Performance

How were troubadour songs performed? As far as the music is concerned, two questions have particularly perplexed both musicologists and modern performers: were the songs rhythmical or not, and were they accompanied by instruments? John Haines concludes that some sort of measured reading already occurred in the very first wave of musical reception, but that these rhythmic interpretations are particular instances, and they are comparatively few; moreover no contemporary witness reports on the issue.[48] For modern performers faced with the problem of how to interpret troubadour tunes, he quotes Margaret Switten: 'To study texts and melodies together is therefore to start from what the manuscripts offer and to evoke an imagined performance. Imagined because we cannot know what an actual performance was like.'[49] Modern performers have taken a variety of approaches, which Haines outlines in some detail,[50] and which Anna Radaelli has described as oscillating essentially between two poles: the legacy of medieval Arabic style espoused by Thomas Binkley in the 1970s based on the concept of authenticity, and the 'impossible authenticities' as defined by Margaret Bent. Radaelli sees this as a sterile debate from a practical point of view.

To medieval listeners the music of a troubadour lyric was part of a dramatic performance. It changed and heightened mood, consolidated social communities and induced appreciation of the skills of composer and soloist – as of course it can also do, in its own way, for a modern audience. But for medieval listeners the lyric was also a poetry of echoes, echoes which transmitted meanings and memories. This has been particularly highlighted by Stefano Milonia's work on musical borrowings. Just as textual study has explored intertextual allusions generated by constellations of rhyme-words and rhyme-endings,[51] so the Italian scholar explores melodic formulae and musical rhymes. We know that medieval poets used rhyme lists as an aid to composition; Milonia suggests that there may have been similar tools for music. These would reside in the memory as a sort of list or collection of melodic cells that can be understood as tools that the poet can utilize and insert into different contexts, just as he or she uses rhyme-words that need to harmonize with the text and the concept to be expressed. He demonstrates how even small melodic cells can be significant if they are united to a textual factor, even without imitation of verse form. So, for example, the intermelodic links he identifies in Raimbaut de Vaqueiras's eulogy to Boniface of Montferrat in 1201 and Guiraut Riquier's *planh* for Amalric IV of Narbonne in 1270, songs which have no direct intertextual connection, not only reinforce Guiraut's praise of the patron to whom he had been faithful for fifteen years but evoke a strong sense of nostalgia for the long-gone golden age of the troubadours.[52]

Some songs were initially designed for performance in particular circumstances or places, for example the Limousin court to which Gaucelm Faidit bids farewell as he leaves on crusade, or the intervention of Raimbaut de Vaqueiras in negotiations over Boniface's position in Thessalonica through a hard-hitting *sirventes*, in an attempt to bypass the influence of the emperor's privy council.[53] The dramatic aspect of performance also involved characters: singers on stage playing a part. Troubadours presented personae: Marcabru mainly comes across as a fire-and-brimstone preacher, but his use of the grammatical first-person veils multiple roles. Role-play is especially clear in the dialogue genres.[54]

In the *partimen* the second speaker may be obliged to defend a point of view quite different from the one usually adopted in his or her songs. In one *tenso*, which has no such constraints, Bernart de Ventadorn and Peire d'Alvernhe playfully reverse their usual roles. Many of the dialogues involve fictive or ventriloquized characters (quite apart from imaginary ones, such as a horse or a coat). At least one may be a 'dialogue of the dead', with unknown troubadours imitating the voices of two of their deceased predecessors. An exchange between 'Lady H' and 'Rofin' appears to be the mocking ventriloquization of a woman celebrated by a rival troubadour and a famous jurist known for his pronouncements on sexual transgressions.[55] It is no great stretch of the imagination to envisage some performances staged with accessories such as hats, costumes, masks or make-up.

Play or playfulness is integral to troubadour culture as a whole. The Occitan tradition of entertainment and sociability blends the two opposites of *sen* and *foudat*, seriousness and folly. In about 1200 Raimon de Miraval advised Forniers, who wanted to become a jongleur, 'to mix acts of wisdom with acts of folly, for a man who is too wise has little worth among men of high reputation'.[56] Guiraut de Borneil puts it more solemnly than most, at a time of European soul-searching and upheaval after the fall of Jerusalem in 1187: 'I neither delight in excessive seriousness nor aim for too much playful folly. However, seriousness, worth and folly all have their time and place if one combines and chooses them well.'[57] Raimbaut d'Aurenga's poems are shot through with the mercurial mood-switches and linguistic playfulness of a jongleur,[58] while Peire Vidal takes *foudat* to comical extremes, posturing as a swaggering warrior who can recapture the Sepulchre single-handedly.[59] Indeed the contradictory tones of the 'first troubadour', Guilhem IX, have been encapsulated in terms of *sen* and *foudat*,[60] as we shall see in the next chapter.

Guilhem IX, historiated initial from *Recueil des poésies des troubadours*, 13th century.

ONE

Guilhem IX

The 'first troubadour', the 7th Count of Poitou and 9th Duke of Aquitaine from 1086 to 1126, was a powerful nobleman ruling territory that far exceeded that of the king of France. He was therefore independent of any need to seek material reward or patronage, even if his songs may have contributed to his social capital and the reputation and cohesion of his court. From a family of secular rulers that prized education and learning, Guilhem may have had some familiarity with the Latin culture, ideas and poetry of contemporary philosophers and theologians.[1] His highly original, entertaining and varied poems include burlesque songs that address an audience of 'companions', no doubt male only, drawing on traditions of both learned rhetoric and jongleuresque ribaldry; others, while highly individual, are more courtly in their treatment of sexual desire and suggest a mixed audience, including noble women and girls. One is a farewell to the world, and an appeal to nobles in and beyond his territory to protect the young son he leaves behind.[2]

Contemporary charters illuminate some of his qualities as a ruler and military leader. They show him as traditional in his methods, and give some idea of the enormous territorial extent and range of his ducal authority and interests, as he moved around his domains surrounded by individuals from a wide range of both lay and ecclesiastical social groups. The chronicle of Saint-Maixent claims that 'he marvellously outshone all princes of the world in the excellence of secular warfare,' and notes many successful engagements in regional conflicts. Other contemporary sources also present a favourable picture of him as a *saecularis miles*.[3]

The duke led a number of armed expeditions against Islam. An early campaign against the Moors in Iberia (1087–9), apparently motivated by aristocratic military honour rather than spiritual purpose, was unsuccessful.[4] At the time of the First Crusade, despite the enormous contingent of southerners following Raymond of Saint-Gilles to Jerusalem, he did not take part in the main expedition, probably because he had as yet no heir,[5] but he led his own crusade in 1101. After a gruelling march through summer heat and the devasted countryside of Anatolia, his army was ambushed and almost entirely wiped out. He managed to escape with a few followers and make his way to Jerusalem, where he fulfilled his vows. In contrast to this crusading failure in the Holy Land, he shared in what the Saint-Maixent chronicle described as a great victory at the battle of Cutanda in June 1120:

> Count William, duke of the Aquitanians, and the king of Aragon fought with Abraham (Ibrahim) and four other Spanish kings on the field of Cutanda; and they conquered and killed 15,000 Moabites and made innumerable prisoners. They captured 2,000 camels and other beasts without number, and they subjugated many castles.[6]

Medieval chroniclers, all churchmen, give him mixed reviews. As might be expected, local establishments praise his character and achievements. A funeral panegyric from the abbey of Sainte-Croix de Talmont extols him as a 'mirror of all probity' and lauds his 'outstanding virtues', his

> boundless strength, vigour and universal human generosity, even to the point of impoverishing himself . . . This was especially true of his knowledge of men's lives, their actions and customs, for he understood every motive and every emotion of the human soul, so that he was never seen to lose his temper unjustly or pity anyone misguidedly.[7]

Others, in marked contrast, 'show a certain relish in the description of his "vicious and impious life"'.[8] Guibert of Nogent, before 1112, stated that after taking the cross the duke recruited not only a conventional force but 'swarms of girls'.[9] William of Malmesbury, writing 25 years after the duke's crusade, described him as 'a fool and a lecher' and claimed he founded a convent of prostitutes near Niort and that he had the image of a viscountess painted on his shield because he wanted to bear her into battle as she used to bear him in bed. On returning from Jerusalem, the chronicler maintained, 'he wallowed in every hogpool of vice, as if he thought that everything was driven by chance rather than ruled by Providence. Spicing his inanities with a certain witty elegance he turned everything into a joke and set his audience roaring with unbridled laughter.'[10]

As Aurell observes, such comments reveal more about the chroniclers' preconceptions than the troubadour. Malmesbury must have known about the troubadour's more salacious songs, but such tirades against his alleged immorality were the prisoner of a traditional moralizing rhetoric that sought to explain the failure of any crusade willed by God and ratified by the pope as the consequence of man's sins, an explanation to which Guibert de Nogent and Geoffrey of Vigeois similarly resort. Such lurid stories should not be taken at face value.[11]

Of the same generation and intellectual background as Malmesbury, Orderic Vitalis offers a shrewder if somewhat ambiguous assessment of the duke: 'He was a bold and upright man and so exceedingly [excessively?] jocose [*iocundus*] that he could outdo even the wittiest minstrels [*facetos . . . histriones*] with his many jests.'[12] It is hard to be sure whether Orderic implied any criticism of Guilhem's burlesque humour here. As Aurell has observed, *histriones* can have strongly pejorative overtones, recalling their use of immoderate language and gestures; yet *facetus*, while it can suggest frivolous joking, is also synonymous with elegance or courtliness. Orderic certainly appreciated Guilhem's literary and performance skills: 'Once returned to prosperity, being a jovial [*iocundus*] and witty [*lepidus*] man, he often recited the trials of his captivity [*captiuitatis*] in the company of kings and magnates and throngs of Christians, using rhythmic verses with skilful modulations.'[13] The epithet *iocundus* in both quotations echoes Guilhem's poetic celebration of joy. However, he was never a prisoner and scholars have tried to explain this report in various ways, such as a knowledge of lost songs or confusion with the narrative *Les Chétifs*, or an interpretation of *captiuitatis* as 'wretched state'.[14] As for his 'rhythmic verses' (*rythmicis versibus*), this expression may indicate a closeness to and prestige associated with learned Latin songs.[15]

The thirteenth-century *vida*,[16] clearly inaccurate in calling Eleanor of Aquitaine Guilhem's daughter rather than granddaughter, concurs with the chronicles as far as his womanizing, military prowess and artistic excellence are concerned: 'The count of Poitiers was one of the courtliest men in the world and one of the greatest deceivers of ladies. He was a fine knight at arms and generous in his wooing; and he was good at composing and singing. And he spent a long time travelling through the world in order to trick ladies.'

While these sources testify to Guilhem's reputation, they need to be approached with caution. This is particularly true of ecclesiastical accounts of Guilhem's various clashes with the Church hierarchy. One such confrontation occurred in 1100 at the Council of Poitiers when the duke, faithful to his overlord Philip I of France, openly defended him during discussion of the king's excommunication for adultery. Philip had repudiated his first wife and married Bertrade de Montfort, the wife of one of his vassals, apparently with his agreement. Lay rulers expected to be able to make their own strategic alliances without Church interference, but at this time reforming clergy were moving to take control of the aristocracy's traditional marriage practices, which demanded a flexible response to shifting political and social situations through the possibility of divorce and remarriage.[17] Another conflict led to the duke himself being excommunicated for refusing to end an adulterous affair with the wife of a certain viscount. After carefully disentangling the evidence Ruth Harvey has concluded: 'It would be legitimate to ask whether the excommunication which began in 1114 and ended in 1117 was really over a mere concubine, or whether it was not more likely to have been over a more practical issue altogether,

Palace of Poitiers, built between the 12th and 13th centuries.

such as ducal control over ecclesiastical appointments or revenues.' Her investigations also undermine the still widespread belief that Guilhem had two wives.[18] Despite his clashes with particular bishops, Guilhem was the Church's constant patron and protector within his domains, making numerous regular grants and concessions to religious establishments throughout his rule and supporting an unbroken series of *magistri scholarum* at the collegiate church of Saint-Hilaire and the cathedral chapter in Poitiers. His piety seems to have been quite traditional[19] – though this did not preclude irreverence towards members of the clergy, or independence of mind.

Burlesque songs

Guilhem's burlesque songs are the ones most likely to have fed into clerical accusations of dissoluteness, and even into his *vida*'s remark that he was 'a great lover of ladies'. Three are addressed to his 'companions'. This implies exclusively male listeners, together with the congenial effacement of social differences within the male group – though questions of hierarchy surface as a poem unfolds.[20]

One piece plays wittily on several ideas: social propriety and hierarchy; the mixing of sense and folly that becomes so integral to the troubadour tradition of courtly sociability and entertainment; and the division of the audience into the knowing in-group and the uncourtly dimwits. 'Companions, I shall compose a suitable/decorous *vers*, and in it there will be more folly than sense, and it will be all mixed up with love and joy and youth. And I consider as a boor anyone who does not listen to/understand it, and willingly learn it by heart' (1, 1–5). The troubadour announces that he has two good horses keen for combat and available for riding, but they can't stand each other; if he could tame them to his liking he would not want to take his 'equipment' anywhere else, for he would be better mounted than any other man. Suggestive ambiguity is blown apart when Guilhem reveals what he has been talking about all along: 'Knights, give me advice on what is bothering me: I have never been so confused about a choice. I don't know which one to settle for – lady Agnes or lady Arsen' (vv. 22–4). These 'mounts' have the same names as the wives of two lords, those of Gimel and Niol, and the last stanza explodes any pretence of male egalitarianism: 'I own the castle and territory of Gimel, and for Niol I am proud in front of everyone, for both are sworn and pledged to me by oath.' If Gimel and Niol are in the Limousin, as Bond has argued, this is likely to be a joke at the expense of Guilhem's vassal, friend and rival there, the Viscount Eble II of Ventadour, with whom he competed in displays of courtly extravagance.[21]

The most obscene of the three 'companion' songs suggests an after-dinner comedy entertainment. It begins with the words 'Companions, I have had such awful hospitality' – a surprising way of thanking one's host! – 'that I cannot help singing and being concerned.' It goes on to suggest a serious and somewhat mysterious subject – 'but I don't want people to know my concerns in many things': namely, 'I don't like a guarded cunt or a pond without fish.' Guilhem solemnly invokes God on the topic: 'Lord God, Who are head and king of the world, why didn't the one who first guarded a cunt die on the spot? For there never was a worse service or guard for one's lady' (III, 7–9). And he expatiates, ever more outrageously, on the 'law of the cunt'. The practice of setting a guard on women's chastity is the target of the third 'companions' song (II), treated in a more serious fashion. Guilhem points out that all guards sleep sometimes, and that if a lady has no access to a lover of the best quality she'll look for satisfaction from the base guards around her: 'if she can't have a charger she'll buy a palfrey', and 'if she's malevolently forbidden strong wine' she'll 'drink water rather than let herself die of thirst'.

Two other compositions exploit jongleuresque ribaldry in different and inventive ways. Through dexterous wordplay, ambivalence and ambiguity, a *gap* or boast interweaves three semantic layers: poetic craftsmanship (signalled by allusions to the colours and flowers of rhetoric),[22] sexual performance and dice-playing:

> I want most people to know whether my *vers* is of a
> good colour, which I have drawn from my workshop;
> for I bear the flower in this craft, and this is the truth,
> and I can produce the *vers* as a witness to this when it
> is laced together. I am also well aware of sense and folly,
> and I recognise shame and fear; and if you propose a game
> of love to me, I am not so stupid that I wouldn't know
> how to choose the best from the bad. (VI, 1–14)

He boasts that he never failed in playing all games 'on a cushion', and that he is so experienced that he has a better 'hand' than anyone at playing the 'sweet game': he is such an 'assured master' that no girlfriend will have him for one night without wanting him again the next – he can earn his 'bread' (a standard medieval metaphor for sex) in all markets! The song ends with a romp in which he relates that the woman he was 'playing' with the other day accused him of having minuscule 'dice' and invited him to another game, which apparently ended in success, though the language is so problematic that it might be the contrary and there is a tradition among later troubadours of undermining comic sexual boasts with professions of impotence.

The remaining burlesque piece (*Farai un vers pos mi sonelh*, BdT 183.12) stages a comical sexual adventure that the troubadour claims to compose while dozing in the hot sun. Wandering alone through the Auvergne as a pilgrim, he claims he encounters two friendly 'ladies' and pretends to be dumb. This induces them to think they have found exactly what they are looking for: a man incapable of revealing their identity (a joke on the courtly emphasis on secrecy in love). They invite him in, sit him by the fire and feed him delicious capons thickly coated with pepper, white bread and fine wine. But to ensure he is not tricking them they bring in a huge ginger cat, which they hold by its tail, dragging the wildly scratching beast down the full length of his naked body. Despite his hundred or more wounds he speaks not a word. Reassured, they prepare for a bath and pleasure, whereupon 'I fucked them so much, as you will hear: one hundred and eighty-eight times, that I nearly broke my straps and my harness; and I can't tell you how ill I was, I ached so much' (v, 79–84).

Guilhem's burlesque songs no doubt fed into the censorious side of his later moral reputation; this last one may even have inspired the *vida*'s naive remark that he 'spent a long time travelling through the world in order to trick ladies'. Malmesbury concedes that his audience laughed a lot.

'Courtly' songs

Burlesque was not his only style, however. Guilhem's love songs are some of the most delicate and moving of the entire troubadour tradition. They relate in interesting ways to the conventions of later troubadour love lyrics, as if these conventions are already in circulation. Guilhem's take on them is his own. *Ab la dolchor del temps novel* (x) blends motifs common to the later troubadour tradition – the spring opening, the lover's hope for a message from his beloved, his timidity, gossips that threaten the success of love, the use of a *senhal* or name concealing the beloved's identity – with exquisite imagery, delicacy of feeling and the celebration of sexual fulfilment: the real thing and not some boastful fantasy.

With the sweetness of the new season
the woods come into leaf, and the birds
sing, each in their own language:
then it is right that one should enjoy
what one most desires.

From the place which most pleases me
I see no messenger or sealed message,
wherefore I neither sleep nor laugh,
nor do I dare to move forward
until I know for sure what will come of it:
whether things will be as I ask.

Our love goes
as the branch of the hawthorn,
which stays trembling on the tree
at night, with the rain and the frost,
until the next day, when the sun spreads its rays
through the green leaves on the twigs.

I still remember a morning
when we brought an end to our war,
and she gave me such a great gift:
her love and her ring.
God let me live long enough
so that I can have my hands under her cloak!

I have no concern that unpleasant talk
will part me from my Good Neighbour,
for I know how gossip circulates
when a few words are spoken.
Some go boasting of love;
we have the piece and the knife.

If Guilhem disparages empty boasting in others, in another joyful 'courtly' song he makes a light joke of his own propensity for boasting.[23]

Most joyously I embark on loving
a joy from which I wish most to be satisfied;
and since I wish to revert to joy
I ought, if possible, to go to the best:
for I love the best, beyond imagining,
that anyone could see or hear of.

I, as you know, ought not to boast,
nor am I good at furnishing myself with great praises;
but if any joy could ever blossom,
this one must above all bear fruit
and shine forth beyond the others
just as the dark day is accustomed to turn bright. (IX, 1–12)

The ambivalent words 'beyond imagining' (*estiers cujar*) suggest the inexpressibility of this wonderful, extraordinary joy, but at the same time its reality, for it is not something simply belonging to the imagination; it could equally be translated as 'without presumption', another light joke at his own expense. Guilhem's nuanced wordplay is not confined to his burlesque songs.

A later emphasis on love as a source of moral improvement is often seen as a key element of what the troubadours call *fin' amors* and we have come to call 'courtly love'. It has been formulated as 'a type of sensual love', in which 'what distinguishes it from other forms of sexual love, from mere passion, from so-called Platonic love, from married love is its purpose or motive, its formal object, namely, the lover's progress and growth in natural goodness, merit and worth.'[24] From this perspective, Guilhem presents but an embryonic, or individual, form of *fin'amors*. The joy his lady inspires is utterly transformative – but in all kinds of ways, some dangerous. It can make a sick man well, but her anger can make a well man die, a sane one go mad, a handsome one lose his looks and the courtliest man become a boor – and all boors turn courtly. For him joy of his lady is a source of perpetual life which he, ever the powerful lord, wants for himself: 'I want to retain her for my own benefit to refresh my heart within me and to renew my flesh so that I may not grow old' (IX, 33–6).

The penultimate stanza suggests the presence of love conventions with which this baron seems to treat as demanding a kind of negotiation or pact: 'If my lady is willing to give me her love, I am ready to take it and be thankful for it, and conceal it and speak sweetly of it, and say and do what pleases her, and cherish her reputation and promote her praise' (37–42). It is as if he is drawing an acknowledged code of courting into the kind of relationship between political allies habitual to him as a lord – even if in the final stanza he professes timidity and deference to her decision.

Such awareness of love conventions surfaces again in *Pos vezem de novel florir*, which sets out what is required of a truly courtly lover. Because it is springtime, he begins, each man ought to 'enjoy the joy that makes him joyful'. It is hard to know whether he is speaking from personal experience or using the grammatical first person as a rhetorical device to present an exemplary illustration of what brings about failure in love.[25] 'Of love I must say nothing but good. Why do I have little or nothing from it? Perhaps because I deserve no more! Yet readily it gives great joy to one who truly holds the rights to it' (VII, 7–12). What is needed for success, he declares, is patience, submission to love's demands, an accommodating manner to strangers and neighbours, willingness to perform services for them, pleasing deeds and polite speech at court. This code of courtesy is bound up with the artistic excellence of the song's words and melody, and connoisseurship on the part of the audience: 'Of the *vers* I tell you that it is worth more to one who understands it well, and it is praised more as a result: for the words are all fashioned evenly to complement each other, and the melody – and I give myself the credit for this – is a good one of fine quality' (37–42). That he presents himself as an authority on love's conventions, sending the song to a certain Stephen in Narbonne, suggests that he is aware of, and intervening in, contemporary discussions on such matters, but not that he invented them.[26] This is just one articulation of a possible 'code' of love. There is no single, excusive set of rules for courtly love or *fin'amors*, any more than there is a single medieval code of chivalry.

Pos de chantar m'es pres talenz

Guilhem sums up his own life in his remarkable farewell to the world (XI). Still known in some form in the early fourteenth century, it was composed when he thought he was about to die.[27] Calm, dignified, plangent, it looks back on a life of service to God and king:

> Since the desire to sing has come upon me
> I shall compose a *vers* for which I grieve.
> No more shall I serve God and king
> in Poitou or the Limousin.
>
> For I will now go into exile
> in great fear, in great peril:
> I shall leave my son in war;
> his neighbours will do him harm.
>
> The departure is so painful for me
> from the seigneury of Poitou!

I leave under Fulk of Anjou's guard
all the land of/and his cousin.

If Fulk of Anjou does not help him,
and the king from whom I hold my estates,
all and sundry will do him harm:
treacherous Gascons and Angevins.

If he is not very wise and valiant
when I have departed from you,
they will soon bring him low,
for they will see he is young and weak.

The historical circumstances are uncertain. Fulk of Anjou may have been Fulk IV le Rechin, with whom Guilhem was apparently on good terms, or else his son, the more hostile Fulk V. The word 'guard' (*garda*) is ambiguous: it could mean 'custody', as some recent editors have thought, or else the vaguer 'protection', and the manuscripts differ as to whether it applies to his son's person as well as his lands. What is clear is that in both cases there is a threat from 'treacherous Angevins'. If his relationship with the count is hostile, Guilhem may be attempting to mitigate it by impressing on him a sense of responsibility towards the boy, whom he tactically refers to as Fulk's kinsman.[28]

He continues by asking forgiveness of anyone, or a particular companion, he has injured in any way:

I beg mercy of my companion:
if I ever wronged him, may he forgive me for it,
and may he pray to Lord Jesus in heaven
in romance and His Latin tongue.

The singular 'companion', possibly synecdochal, allows for the possibility that he is still referring to Fulk, with whom he is attempting an act of reconciliation.

Finally, he contemplates his own death with dignity and the self-assurance of one who expects peace in the afterlife. His earthly life he sums up, without apology, as one of *proeza* and *joi*. *Proeza* can mean many things, but here it refers above all to knightly deeds or *cavalaria* (which is not the same thing as 'chivalry', a later development).[29]

I belonged to prowess and joy,
but now we part from each other;
and I shall go away to Him
in Whom all sinners find peace.

I have let go of all I used to love,
a life of knightly deeds and pride;
and since it pleases God, I embrace it all,
and pray Him to retain me for His own.

All my friends I beg at death
to come together and do me great honour;
for I have had joy and sport
far and near and in my own home.

Thus I abandon joy and sport
and squirrel and grey furs and sable.

Guilhem's small but many-sided corpus epitomizes the quintessential blend of *sen* and *foudat* that lies at the heart of troubadour poetry. His poetic successors may not always have approved of him, but they were much in his debt.

Jaufre Rudel, historiated initial from a *Chansonnier provençal* manuscript, 13th century.

TWO

Jaufre Rudel

Jaufre sings of love alone – of the dreamy love his contemporary Marcabru despised. He is not a wordsmith of the kind represented by Guilhem IX or Marcabru, or the later Arnaut Daniel, the supreme craftsman of *trobar car*, who dazzled and intrigued his audience with rare rhymes, complex forms and interwoven levels of meaning. This may explain why the thirteenth-century *vida* writer described his words as 'poor'.[1] A self-conscious craftsman of a different stamp, however, he shares with other troubadours such as Marcabru the claim that the more you listen to his song the more it is worth.[2] Jaufre's *art poétique* contains an added emphasis on musical performance:

> No-one knows how to sing if he cannot sing in tune,
> or compose a poem (*vers*) if he cannot fashion words,
> or know how things work in a song
> if he does not understand the theme within himself.
> But my song begins like this:
> the more you hear it, the more it will be worth . . .
>
> The *vers* is good, for I have committed no fault in it
> and everything that is in it is fitting;
> and the one who learns it from me
> should take care not to break or fragment it. (I, 1–6, 31–4)

The 'one who learns it from me' could be anyone in the audience, but is more likely to be the jongleur who will take it to the named recipients in the Quercy and the Toulousain (35–6). The lines highlight the collaboration of composer and jongleur in creation, transmission and performance.

Jaufre and Guilhem IX

Jaufre belonged to the family of the lords of Blaye who had taken over control of the fortress of Blaye on the Gironde in the 1030s. In the 1060s the family entered into alliance with the Duke of Aquitaine, William VIII. One of the latter's chief advisers was the troubadour Jaufre Rudel's grandfather, William Fredeland of Blaye (d. *c.* 1101), who bore the title 'prince of Blaye', a name the duke gave to a number of his vassals and which was apparently in vogue in nearby Saintonge at the time.[3] In the 1120s alliances changed. According to the only source for the period, between 1120 and 1126 Guilhem IX set siege to Blaye and destroyed its walls and keep. Shortly afterwards the Count of Angoulême, Vulgrin II (d. 1140), rebuilt the whole castle and gave it back to the Rudel family, but during the mid-1120s found himself facing a rebellion by Girard I of Blaye (d. 1127), the troubadour Jaufre's father, over a dispute concerning another castle. Girard was supported by a number of local lords who feared the expansionist ambitions of the Count of Angoulême, whose ally was Guilhem IX (d. 1126). One of these local lords was Hugh Brun of Lusignan, to whom Jaufre sent *Quan lo rius de la fontana* (III, 32).[4]

Although the lords of Blaye enjoyed a variety of seigneurial powers and revenues that enabled them to maintain a vassalic clientele and *milites*, the troubadour could not have benefited from these as lord of Blaye, or lived there during Guilhem's lifetime, since he succeeded his father Girard only after the latter's death in 1127, and may not even have taken over the lordship until as late as 1140. Jaufre has been referred to by modern scholars as a 'prince without a castle', a 'marginal man', with theories constructed around this idea about the nature of his poetry,[5] though we do not actually know how long his exile from Blaye lasted or how the dates of composition of his surviving six songs relate to this.

Jaufre and the Second Crusade

We do know that Jaufre went on the Second Crusade, since the troubadour Marcabru sent one of his songs to him *outra mar*. He may have died there. Unless he perished on the voyage, he must have arrived in Acre with the other southern crusaders in April 1148. By the thirteenth century there started to form a legend of Jaufre falling in love with the Countess of Tripoli and dying in her arms, which crystallized in his *vida*:[6]

> Jaufre Rudel of Blaye was a very noble man, prince of Blaye. And he fell in love with the countess of Tripoli without seeing her, because of the good things he had heard about her from the pilgrims who came from Antioch. And he made many songs about her with good tunes and poor words. And out of a desire to see her he took the cross and set out on the sea, and fell ill on the ship, and was brought to Tripoli, to an inn, as if dead. And the countess was informed of this and she came to him, to his bed, and took him in her arms. And he knew that she was the countess, and recovered his hearing and his breath, and praised God for sustaining his life until he saw her; and thus he died in her arms. And she had him buried in great honour in the house of the Temple; and then, on that day, she became a nun for the grief she had for his death.[7]

Death of Jaufre Rudel, historiated initial from *Recueil des poésies des troubadours*, 13th century.

This is an imaginative attempt to explain in narrative form the central theme of Jaufre's poetry, *amor de lonh*. The expression could be translated in various ways, such as 'love from afar', 'far-off/faraway/distant love' or 'love at a distance'. Persisting into modern times and giving rise to such recreations as an opera by the Finnish composer Kaija Saariaho and Lebanese librettist Amin Maalouf,[8] the legend bears witness to the hypnotic suggestiveness of Jaufre's love poetry, and its particular, haunting evocation of a love whose very vagueness opens it to multifarious interpretations.

Amor de lonh

Jaufre's *amor de lonh* is epitomized in his best-known song, *Lan qand li jorn son lonc en mai* (IV). The text used as the basis for the English translation here was edited by the Swiss scholar François Zufferey, who carried out an extremely thorough analysis of the complex relationship between the many manuscripts with the aim of arriving at the best approximation of the original text, composed some century and a half before them.[9] The manuscript disparities show that the text was much subject to change, so that the various past audiences, and modern readers relying on other editions, have interpreted it differently.

I Now that the days are long in May
the sweet song pleases me of distant birds,
but as I am separated from there
I remember a far-off love.
I go despondent and bowed down from longing,
so that neither song nor hawthorn flower
pleases me more than frozen winter.

II Never will I know the joy of love
if I know not joy of this far-off love:
for none I know gracious or better
anywhere, either near or far.
So true and sure is her worth
that there in the realm of the Saracens
would that I were called captive for her sake!

III Sorrowful and joyful will I depart
when I go to see the far-off love;
but when I'll see her I know not,
for our lands are too far apart.
Many are the passes and paths there,
and for that reason I cannot see the future,
but may all be as it pleases God!

IV Joy will appear when I ask her
for the far-off love, for love of God,
and if it pleases her, I'll lodge
nearby to her, though from afar.

Then the discourse will appear refined
when, as a distant lover, I shall be so close
that with fine words I shall know the joy
of courtly company.[10]

V Assuredly I hold the Lord as true
through Whom I'll see the far-off love;
but for one good that falls to me
I have two ills, for it is so far off.
Ah! would I were a pilgrim there
so that my staff and cloak
were gazed on by her lovely eyes!

VI God who made all that comes and goes
and made firm this far-off love,
grant me the power, for it is my desire,
that I may soon see this far-off love
in reality, in such appropriate places
that the chamber and the garden
would be forever like a palace for me.

VII He speaks the truth who calls me avid
and craving for far-off love,
for no other joy pleases me so much
as the joy of far-off love.
But what I wish is so deferred for me,[11]
for my godfather fated me
to love and be not loved.

VIII Since what I wish is so deferred for me,
an outright curse on the godfather
who fated I should be not loved!

Each stanza follows the same rhyme scheme and repeats the refrain-word *lonh* (spelled *loing* in Zufferey's base manuscript and hence edition) in the second and fourth lines of each.

I Lan qand li jorn son lonc en mai
m'es bels douz chans d'auzels de loing,
e quan me sui partitz de lai
remembra.m d'un amor de loing:
vau de talan embroncs e clis,
si que chans ni flors d'albespis
no.m platz plus que l'iverns gelatz.

The literature on this enigmatic *amor de lonh*, and the *amor de terra lonhdana* (love from a distant land) of *Quan lo rius de la fontana* (III, 8), is extensive. It has been interpreted as love for the Virgin Mary, or for the Holy Land; as a manifestation of the 'paradoxe amoureux' allegedly underlying all troubadour poetry, a 'love which does not wish to possess, but to take pleasure in this state of non-possession'; as Christian love transposed onto the secular plane; as simple nostalgia, or love of God, or pure, refined love as opposed to carnal love; or as love as a reflection of the socioeconomic situation of landless knights and sublimation of their desire for marriage to a high-born lady.[12]

The love object is enigmatic. After a conventional spring opening in a winter variant, the poetic 'I' introduces the lady herself in the form of *lieis*, 'her', though since *amor* in medieval Occitan is grammatically feminine there is a blurring in the song between love and the *domna* (courtly lady, the powerful feminized form of *dominus* or lord). The reference to being a pilgrim in the realm of the Saracens suggests a possible, but not at all necessary, connection with crusading. The idea of being a prisoner for love is a troubadour commonplace, but why would he like to be called a captive for her sake in the land of the Saracens?[13]

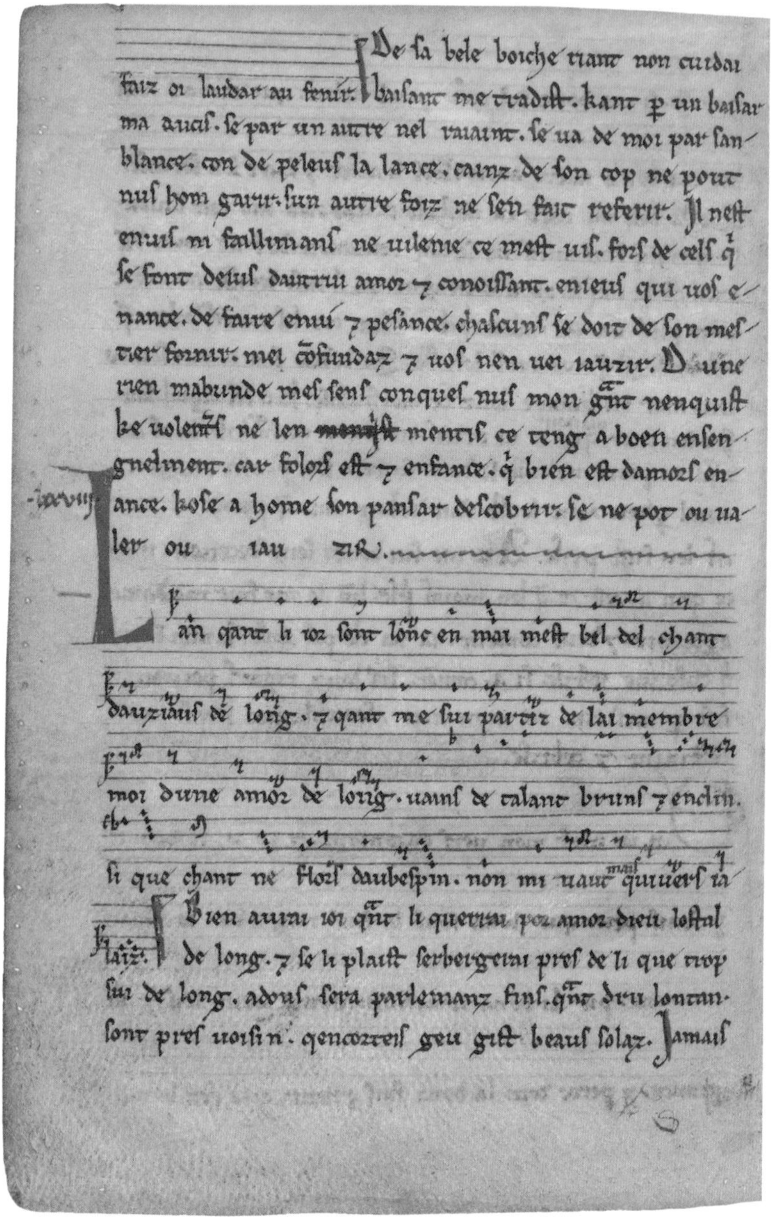

Lan qand li jorn son lonc en mai, musical notation from *Chansonnier de Saint-Germain des Prés*, 13th century.

Would he like to dedicate his crusading to her? Does she, as the *vida* author related, live there? Or is this all, as some have thought, an allegory?

As the poetic 'I' imagines the joy of finally coming into the woman's presence, the intimacy he seeks, while involving physical proximity, interestingly takes the form of *words*: the *paraulas* (the exchange of words) will be *fis*: an adjective combining the meanings of pure, true, noble, refined; and *solatz* refers to the pleasures of courtly company and conversation.

Throughout the song the speaker invokes God: all will be as it pleases Him; the speaker will ask for her love 'for the love of God'; the Lord will enable him to see the *amor de lonh*, and created it along with 'all that comes and goes'. The chamber and garden that are the usual places for lovemaking belong to a commonplace trope of medieval literature, the so-called *hortus conclusus* or 'enclosed garden', linked to commentaries on the biblical Song of Songs that identify it with the Virgin's womb, or the paradise of union between the soul or the Church and Christ.[14] Is Jaufre, as other troubadours who also invoke the help of God in obtaining their desires, skirting blasphemy in involving God in extramarital love, or is his love purely spiritual, or mystical, and linked to the Second Crusade?[15]

Zufferey sets these speculations aside, arguing that there is nothing in the song to suggest that the speaker has a crusade in mind, that the staff and cloak are characteristic of a pilgrim rather than a crusader, and that the birds from afar in May are likely to be migrating from the south rather than the east: an interpretation he regards as supported by the reference to *portz* or mountain passes in verse 19, though in fact the word could equally refer to the ports or the mountain passes on the way to the Holy Land.[16] Emphasizing the need for great attentiveness to linguistic detail, he concludes that the song really is, as the *vida* author believed, about love for a far-off woman to whom the lyric 'I' wants to journey as a poor pilgrim, the voyage is not to the East but a pilgrimage to Spain from where the *auzelhs de lonh* come, and the poem deals with the theme of impossible love where the lover's only recourse is the exaltation of desire and a waking dream.[17] There is much to recommend this interpretation, though it is well to recall 'the multivalence of the love-language itself, the imagery that hovers between sensuality and mysticism, or indeed bridges them'.[18]

A political reading brings the delicate and allusive poetry crashing to earth. Sébastien-Abel Laurent links Jaufre's poetry to his rebellion against Guilhem IX, and hypothesizes that the object of his desire was Guilhem's daughter Agnes. This noblewoman, Laurent argues, would have been a highly valuable match, potentially accessible to him by virtue of his rank, but denied to him by the duke. He identifies the duke with the 'godfather' (*pairis*) of the song, and the 'brother' (*fraire*) and 'sister' (*seror*) of *Belhs m'es l'estius e.l temps floriz* with the duke's son Guilhem X and the more complaisant Agnes: 'all that the brother denies me I hear granted by the sister' (V, 45–6). The poetic theme of *amor de lonh*, he suggests, could have been motivated by a form of political rancour.[19] However reductive this interpretation, it has the merit of offering a possible explanation of the mysterious *pairis*, *fraire* and *seror*.

After Jaufre the theme of *amor de lonh* continues to resonate throughout the troubadour tradition, as poets lament the distance keeping lovers apart: whether as a result of the social impediments of the *lauzengiers* and *gilos*, or from the disdainful object of the speaker's love, or indeed from geographical separation, in the case of crusade songs.[20] But Jaufre's contemporary Marcabru was unimpressed. In his song *Ans que·l terminis verdei* he attacked crusaders who allowed themselves to be duped by 'lurve':

Before the season grows green,
I shall sing and rightly so.
Whoever may be cheered by love,
I get from it not a thing.
On any man who goes courting
I wish no more noxious illness.
Anyone under love's tyranny
is sure to starve and freeze to death![21]

This diatribe against female venality and male, lust-driven gullibility concludes with the warning that 'the man whom love will deceive should never sign himself with the cross (become a crusader)': a possible jibe at Jaufre himself.

Jaufre's *Quan lo rossinhols el foillos* (VI) contains a final stanza, preserved in five of its thirteen manuscripts, which urges the need to follow Jesus to Bethlehem. Unless it is apocryphal, it is likely to be a call to go on crusade rather than a vaguer one to lead a spiritual life. In this version of the song the poet moves from evocations of the joy of the simple, natural possession of love, to the longing for love not yet possessed, to anxiety and frustration at its non-fulfilment, to a decision to abandon it in favour of a different kind of love.

Love, happily I part from you,
because I go to seek what is best for me;
and I am fortunate, inasmuch
as my heart already rejoices at it;
but on account of my Good Protector,
who wants me and calls me and judges me worthy,
I need to restrain my yearning.

And he who stays in a life of pleasure
and does not follow God to Bethlehem,

how he will ever be valiant I do not know,
or how he can ever achieve salvation;
for I know and firmly believe
that anyone taught by Jesus
can rely on a sure school.

Zufferey ascribes this piece to a later period of Jaufre's compositions, when he abandons the courting of a woman and gives himself to divine love and the crusade. Was he moved by Marcabru's rebukes?[22] We shall never know. But as various commentators have remarked, Jaufre is a poet who deliberately plays on different registers, both sacred and profane, and poetry is by definition enigmatic and polysemic.[23]

THREE

Marcabru

One of the greatest and most influential troubadours, and a remarkably versatile poet and musician, Marcabru was active in the second quarter of the twelfth century.[1] His career began in Poitiers at the court of Guilhem IX's son, William X of Aquitaine. When William died suddenly in Santiago in April 1137 and his daughter Eleanor of Aquitaine married Louis VII of France, the troubadour headed across the Pyrenees to seek his fortune at the courts of Spain, and to support the Reconquista. At the time of the Second Crusade (1147–9) he was back in France. A satirist and a moralist of unknown origin, following in the medieval tradition of clerical misogyny, he slates what he sees as the corruption of noble bloodlines through sexual immorality – an interesting commentary, implied though never explicit, on the ethos expressed in the poems of his patron's father. Yet despite his clerical leanings he is a key figure in the development of secular courtly ideals, especially through his concept of *joven* (youth). In his 44 surviving works, four of which retain their melodies, he adopts a variety of poetic personae, verse forms and poetic styles, drawing attention to his own considerable craft as a wordsmith and conveyor of truth.

Marcabru, historiated initial from a *Chansonnier provençal* manuscript, 13th century.

Name and social condition

There are no external documentary records referring to a Marcabru who can plausibly be identified with our poet, and information about his identity and life has to be deduced – carefully – from the songs themselves.[2] 'Marcabru' is probably a nickname or stage title, like that of his contemporary Cercamon. While the latter's designation seems based on the idea of his wanderings ('he searches the world'), attempts to interpret Marcabru's name through speculative etymology – *bru* for example meaning 'brown' or 'dark' – are inconclusive. His two *vidas* are a mix of literal-minded speculation and simplistic commentary, with some possible grains of actual information. One claims that 'Marcabru was from Gascony, son of a poor woman whose name was Marcabruna, as he says in his song: "Marcabru, the son of lady Bruna, was begotten under such a moon that he knew how love wreaks havoc – Listen! – for he never loved any woman, nor was he loved by one."' He may or may not have been from Gascony, but the rest is literal extrapolation from a song whose precise interpretation eludes us.[3] The other *vida* reports:

> Marcabru was abandoned at a rich man's gate, and no-one knew who he was or from where. And Sir Aldric del Vilar had him brought up. Afterwards he stayed with a troubadour named Cercamon until he himself started to compose. And at that time his name was Pan-Perdut, but from then on his name was Marcabru. And in those days people did not use the term *canso*, but everything that was sung was called *vers*. And he was greatly famed and listened to everywhere, and feared because of his tongue, for he spoke so vituperatively that in the end the castellans of Guyenne whom he had criticised so much put him to death.

The story about Aldric del Vilar is based on a faithful interpretation of two texts, one of which may have been composed by a man of that name, but which may equally have been staged by Marcabru himself.[4] This *vida* provides no basis for seeing him as a man of humble origins and illegitimate birth, though its recognition of his vituperative tongue is fair enough.

In his poems our troubadour identifies himself with the *soudadiers*, men dependent on pay or wages (*souda*), and their lord's generosity. This social category may have included a wide range of retainers such as simple soldiers, young landless knights and other unmarried young men who hired out their services as mercenaries, and troubadours. Marcabru accuses the rich on whom they depend as being miserly in gifts and spirit, and presents *soudadiers* as the upholders of courtly values, particularly *joven*: 'hired men, by whom youth is maintained and joy likewise' (XLIV, 1–2). Courts are universally places of rivalry, of jostling for status and advantage; Marcabru complains that lords favour other servants, such as guards set to watch over the chastity of noble wives and 'foppish courtiers, retainers with a steward's office who spend their time lounging cosily by the fire' and 'obtaining more than the legitimate rewards of their office': 'squatters with their combed-out hair, who are always demanding perks – and they demand this as their due' (XXXIX, 25, 59–61). As Ruth Harvey has argued, Marcabru may be 'abusing men who have become established in the *maisnada* and in the lord's favour and who are blocking access to similar secure positions by the *soudadiers*'.[5]

Was Marcabru a soldier, or a landless younger son of a knightly family? Either is possible. His poems show that he had received some clerical training, and that as well as being familiar with epic material, legends and the compositions of other troubadours he was profoundly influenced by Old Testament misogyny and a hardline, orthodox morality. He is unlikely to have been retained simply in his capacity as a troubadour. Given his clerical training, he (and Cercamon too) may have exercised administrative functions.[6]

'Career', patrons and crusading

Marcabru's songs indicate that he travelled widely in southwest France and northern Spain, visiting the courts of Poitiers, Toulouse, León and Barcelona. As well as William X of Aquitaine his patrons probably included Alfonso Jordan, the Count of Toulouse, Emperor Alfonso VII of Castile-León, and possibly the Count of Barcelona, Ramón Berenguer IV.[7] A reference in poem XIX hints that he visited Saint-Denis in northern France, or at any rate knew someone who had.

In Poitou he supported William X's interests,[8] for example, promoting an armed conflict with the Angevins (VIII), which probably took place in 1130 when William was assisting his kinsman Thibaut de Blaizon against Geoffrey of Anjou. After the duke's death the troubadour sought patronage in 'Castile and towards Portugal, where greetings have never been sent before', and 'towards Barcelona too', lamenting that 'since the Poitevin has failed me, I will ever more be lost like Arthur' (IVb, 55–60). On the way he hoped to find support from a young nobleman in the Béarn: 'I am told that a little one is growing up here in Gascony, towards Ossau, where I may find food if I am lost' (IV, 66–8).[9]

In the winter of 1137–8 he was at the court of Alfonso VII, praising him for his heroic efforts against the Saracens. Introducing himself to the recently crowned emperor, he intertwines crusading exhortation with pointed but oblique references to 'hospitality and generosity', the food and gift-giving on which court retainers depend:

Emperor, of my own accord,
since your prowess is increasing,
I did not delay at all in coming here,
for joy nourishes you, your worth is enhanced,
and youth keeps you vigorous and in good spirits
which causes your valour to grow.

Since the son of God summons you
to avenge Him against Pharaoh's line,
you should indeed rejoice at it;
for beyond the passes [of the Pyrenees] the barons,
    most of them,
lack hospitality and generosity.
May God never let them profit from it!

Since those men over there are neglecting it,
for the good of Spain and the holy sepulchre
you should indeed carry the burden,
and drive the Saracens back,
lay low their lofty pride,
and God will be with you at the end.

The Almoravids take heart
because of the powerful lords beyond the passes,
for these have begun to weave a web
of cloth of envy and of wrong,
and each one says that on his death
he will divest himself of his share. (XXII, 1–30)

The song is one of the earliest manifestations of an approach to the Christian-Muslim conflicts in Spain which sees them in crusading terms, and the earliest response to the crusading movement on the part of Occitan or Old French lyrics. The Almoravids were Berber devotees of an Islamic fundamentalist sect who overran Muslim Spain between about 1090 and 1120. Crusading pilgrims at this time might follow either the *via de Hispania* or the *via Jerusalem* (or indeed both, as Guilhem IX had done); Marcabru, critical of the French 'lords beyond the Pyrenees' who have taken control of Poitou – thus depriving him of a living – promotes the Reconquista as a way of serving God's cause in the Holy Land as well as Spain.

It is impossible to know how successful his approaches to Spanish rulers may have been or how long he stayed in Iberia. At any rate his other song addressed to Alfonso is more explicitly pointed, and grudging:

Emperor, for your great name
and for the prowess that you have,
I have come to you, know this,
and should not need to regret it . . .

If I fail to get any gift from you,
in a pond that he hears praised
never will Marcabru go fishing,
for he would always expect failure. (XXIII, 1–4, 25–8)

Several of his songs allude to the Second Crusade, when he seems to have returned north of the Pyrenees and to be in a position to know who had left for Syria, and to gather news and gossip from pilgrims and crusaders returning from the Latin East. All these allusions are negative, or at least equivocal.[10] He allows a sympathetic character to complain against the French king Louis VII's call to arms (I). As we have seen, Jaufre Rudel went on this crusade, and Marcabru sent poem XV to him, saying, 'I want the French to have it, to cheer their hearts, for God can allow them this, whether it is a sin or a good deed.' The song contains what appears to be a veiled allusion to rumours about Eleanor of Aquitaine's conduct in Syria and, if so, it was unlikely to 'cheer their hearts'. Moreover the final remark may insinuate that these crusaders liked listening to sinful secular songs, though as this one is a condemnation of sin they might not enjoy it anyway.[11] Whatever the case, after the failure of the Second Crusade in 1149, Marcabru returns in his famous *Vers del lavador* (XXXV) to his previous commitment to the Reconquista. Cercamon had promoted the Second Crusade as the opportunity for spiritual

Second Crusade, miniature from *Roman de Godefroi de Bouillon*, 14th century.

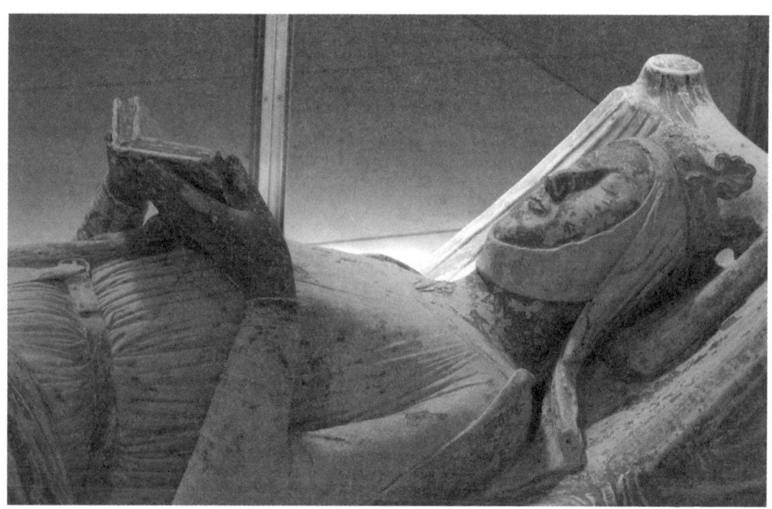

Effigy of Eleanor of Aquitaine, Royal Abbey of Fontevraud, early 13th century.

cleansing: 'Now a man can cleanse and purify himself of great guilt, if he is burdened with it; and if he is brave, he will set out for Edessa and abandon the perilous world, and thereby he can free himself of the burden which causes many to stumble and perish.'[12] In the wake of the crusade's collapse, Marcabru now exhorts men to participate in the campaign led by Ramón Berenguer IV of Barcelona in 1148–9, against Tortosa and Lerida:

> Peace in the name of the Lord!
> Marcabru made the *vers* and the tune.
> Hear what he says:
> how the heavenly Lord
> has created for us in His loving-kindness
> in our vicinity, a washing-place
> such as never was before, except in Outremer
> over there near the valley of Josaphat;
> but it is about the one over here that I exhort you.
> (XXXV, 1–9)

Although he calls on all to avenge God the wrongs being done to Him 'both here and over there towards Damascus', the contrast he draws between the Spanish and the French could hardly be more conspicuous:

> Here [in Guyenne and Poitou] and in Spain the marquis
> and all of Solomon's Temple
> bear the weight
> and the burden of pagan pride,
> for which youth gathers base renown;
> and the public outcry about that other washing-place
> pours down on the highest-ranking leaders:
> broken failures, weary of valour,
> loving neither joy nor delight. (55–63)

On the one hand he lauds Ramón Berenguer (now marquis of Tortosa) and the Templars; on the other he derides the miserable, craven performance of the French leaders, on their way home. After this nothing of our troubadour's career is known for sure.

Misogyny and courtly ideals

Of a generation later than Guilhem IX, Marcabru introduces an ethical dimension into troubadour concepts of love: not as an author of love lyrics but as a satirist and a moralist. His targets are a corrupt aristocracy and venal, lustful women. A misogynist of the first order, he follows in a long antifeminist tradition from Classical antiquity to scripture and the Church Fathers in warning against the dangers posed by feminine greed, wiles and sexual voraciousness:[13]

> You hired men, by whom youth
> is maintained and joy likewise,

hear the wicked arguments
of the false, burning whores!
In a whore, if you put your trust in her,
a man is betrayed;
when the fool thinks she is smiling
he is mocked. (XLIV, 1–8)

Compared to a chimera, a typical image of lust found in medieval church carvings,[14]

The whore seems like a lion at the front:
at the beginning she is fierce with pride,
but then when she has had her way with him
until he droops/abases himself, she couldn't care less.
Often in her whoring
the harlot stinks,
like a rotting carcass
in a slaughterhouse. (17–24)

The whore's rule is to resist the rich man
unless she extracts high rent from him
at the place where she stretches the crossbow open,
where she knows the bread is and expects the wine.
The wily woman full of tricks
acts with wanton greed
when she leaves the noble
and chooses the degenerate. (73–80)

Why should these warnings be directed at the *soudadiers*? Because they are the upholders of courtly values, of joy and youth (XLIV, 1–2); and in this they are opposed to the aristocracy, as Marcabru says elsewhere: 'As long as good youth [*jovens*] was the father of the world and pure love its mother, prowess was maintained, both in private and in public, but now dukes and kings and even an emperor have reduced her to the level of a peasant' (v, 37–42). He attributes the decline of courtly values among aristocrats, particularly their avarice and unwillingness to support the *soudadiers*, to the sexual immorality of adulterous married noblemen engaged in a round of cuckoldry:

> A married man scratching another's cunt
> can be sure his own goes fishing
> and shows how someone mixes his drink
> so as to beat him with his own stick.
> And he'll be wrong to complain about it,
> for right and reason teach us this:
> selling dearly means buying dearly,
> according to the law of Pisa. (xi, 49–56)

Meanwhile noblewomen couple with household menials, corrupting their bloodline with bastards, the 'wicked powerful men, not one of whom provides hospitality or holds court' (xxxi, 46–54). Some of Marcabru's songs are equally virulent against love in the abstract, hardly distinguishable from Woman: 'I'll tell you how love minces: she sings to you and winks at another, she talks with you but gestures to another' (xviii, 19–21); 'Love used to be straight but now she is twisted and chipped, and she has gathered this reputation – listen! – that where she can't bite she licks more roughly than a cat' (25–30); 'He who lives with a woman's wiles is rightly struck down by evil, as the Scripture teaches' (67–9).

Marcabru ran into criticism for his plain, or indeed colourful, speaking. Claiming to compose according to *trobar naturau*, the art of composing according to 'what is backed up by truth', he reports that 'buzzing, petty troubadours with confused thoughts turn [his] song into nothing and make a mockery of it' (xxxiii,

7–12).[15] His reputation for misogyny outlived him: manuscript K's *vida* states that 'He composed miserable *vers* and miserable *sirventes* and he spoke ill of women and of love,' while an anonymous *trobairitz* declares indignantly that 'Sir Marcabru, like a preacher when he is in a church or oratory . . . vilifies the unbelievers, and he vilifies ladies in a similar way; and I say to you that this is not very honourable for one who defames the place from where children are born.'[16]

No doubt in response to criticisms on the part of a public both resistant to his negative fulminations and enthralled by the love songs of his contemporaries such as Cercamon and Jaufre Rudel, Marcabru seeks on several occasions to distinguish between different kinds of love: *fals'amor* or *amar* (a pun on 'loving' and 'bitter') and *fin'amor*.

> Troubadours with the wit of a child
> sow conflict among good people,
> and turn into punishment
> what is backed up by truth,
> and they deliberately make words
> interwoven with corrupt thoughts.
>
> And they put on a single level
> false loving (*fals amar*) and pure love (*amor fina*).
> I say that he who cosies up to *amar*
> makes war on himself,
> for once his purse is empty,
> the fool is a sorry sight. (XXXVII, 7–18)

False love or *amar* he identifies with the singer Eble II, Viscount of Ventadour, who 'upholds his foolish understanding in the face of reason' (XXXI, 73–4). *Fin'amor* he formulates as love based on joy, patience, self-control, mutuality of desire, trust, purity, honesty and freedom from greed (XXXVII, 24–40); courtesy, controlled speech, personal worth and liberality (XXXII, 55–67); and monogamy born of true courtliness:

A man can pride himself on courtliness
if he knows well how to observe moderation,
and someone who wants to hear everything that is said
or aims to possess all that he sees
must needs moderate this 'all',
or he will never be very courtly.

Moderation lies in noble speech,
and courtliness comes from loving;
and anyone who does not want to be misjudged
should guard against all base conduct,
deceitful and wild behaviour;
then he will be wise, even if it might not make
him any happier.

For in this way, a wise man can live well
and a good lady can improve,
but she who takes two or three lovers
and does not want to pledge herself to one alone –
well, her reputation and worth
decrease with every passing month. (XV, 13–30)

His positive formulations are abstract and vague, but insofar as his *fin'amor* involves the love between a man and a woman, it seems close to ideas being elaborated by twelfth-century churchmen on the place of affection in marriage.[17]

Craft

Despite his negative reputation for slander and misogyny, Marcabru undoubtedly made a serious impact on his contemporaries and successors. His poems survive in sixteen of the forty-odd troubadour songbooks, and some eleven later writers refer to him.[18] If the *vida* of manuscript K says he 'composed miserable *vers* and miserable *sirventes* and he spoke ill of women and of love', these words follow the statement that 'he was one of the first troubadours people remember.' Manuscript R begins its massive anthology with his compositions, headlining them with the rubric 'Here begins the song [*so*] of Marcabru who was the first troubadour there was.' His forceful engagement with contemporary debates about love, and his contribution to their development and crystallization, indubitably contributed to this impact. So did his remarkable craft, both musical and verbal.

Although only four melodies survive, two in manuscript R (XVIII and XXX) and two in the 'Frenchified' manuscript W (XIII and XXXV), they are enough to suggest a powerful formal imagination. Musicologists have stressed their individual distinctiveness. Vincent Pollina has described XIII and XXXV as 'cantor's pieces' reminiscent of some Gregorian chant, designed for expert or virtuoso performance, demanding a fairly wide vocal range and frequently employing ornamentation and skips, while suggesting that the other two were designed for an average vocal capacity.[19] Manuscript R's rubric points to the essential aspect of his music – indeed *so* could even be simply translated as 'music', even if the manuscript's first text lacks its musical accompaniment.[20] Further indications of the variety of his musical approach emerge from the troubadour's own words, whether he composes on a *son desviat*, a borrowed tune (V), or a *so vieill antic*, 'age-old air' (XXXII). This 'ancient song' may have been intended to recall *chansons de geste* (there are similarities of versification) or liturgical song.[21] Further evidence of the variety of his musical structures appears in the notable variety of his songs' verse forms, fourteen of which employ schemes not found elsewhere in the troubadour corpus.

His verbal craftsmanship is manifested in a variety of ways. His vocabulary ranges across the customary, the forensic, the learned, the courtly and the obscene. It contains a vast number of rare words, as well as coinages of compounds such as *guasta-pa* (bread-spoilers) or *creba-mostier* (church-wreckers), many satirical or parodic coinages such as *contradenteiar* (to bare one's teeth), as well as special word-formations, tense usages and verb morphology.[22] While his versification sometimes shows rough features such as loose, approximative rhymes, elsewhere it reveals a concern for accuracy and virtuoso proficiency, within restricted parameters such as in the use of rare and/or difficult rhymes. The 58 lines of poem XIV, for example, are entirely constructed on the masculine and feminine forms of rhymes ending in *-ansa/-ans*, *-alh/-alha* and *-esc/esca*, their order alternating in odd and even stanzas.[23]

Marcabru is particularly conscious of the virtues and vices of eloquence, following in the rhetorical traditions of Classical antiquity and the Middle Ages, as well undoubtedly as other less learned traditions. Hostile to the glib, imprecise and corrupting use of words, the 'foolish loquacity' of the uncourtly, the 'sweet speech' of the whore, the way false love 'smoothes out and polishes its words', the boastful exaggerations of the stingy rich and the confused speech and thoughts of his critics and petty love-poets, he himself is expertly versed in the science of *eloquentia* derived directly or indirectly from medieval rhetoric. This appears in many aspects of his use of words: the arrangement of arguments following rhetorical *dispositio*, the appropriation of forensic terms in presenting himself as accuser, defender and inquisitor into a judicial inquiry into the truth about love, the 'binding up' of the theme of a poem or its gradual unfolding, and many kinds of wordplay such as puns, figures of repetition and the use of 'colours' to suggest meanings. His *trobar naturau* broadly reflects a view of nature found in Christian scholasticism, where nature mirrors hidden truth and moral order, requiring wisdom and effort to pierce its outward form and discover its true significance. This he illustrates with copious nature imagery and the use of symbols drawn from the medieval bestiary, herbary and lapidary traditions.[24] His vituperative, polemical eloquence, which includes harsh sounds as well as harsh words, is the model for what later troubadours call *trobar brau*, the rough or harsh style, just as his complex interweaving of words and meanings leads to their development of the *trobar clus* or 'closed' style of composition.

An interesting aspect of Marcabru's poetic craft is his adoption of different personae. The dominant one is 'Marcabru the preacher', referred to later by the anonymous *trobairitz*. This figure is particularly striking at the beginning of *Pax in nomine Domini* (XXXV). It is easy to imagine the troubadour, or another singer, making the appropriate liturgical gestures as he intones this Latin formula. In *Pos mos coratges esclarzis* (XL), where love is closer to the love of God than marital love, presiding over the Day of Judgement, the poetic 'I' is a complex blend of poet-musician, potential sinner and fire-and-brimstone preacher:

Since my heart grows clear
for the joy which makes me rejoice,
and I see that love divides and chooses,
which makes me hope to be enriched,
I must purify my whole song
so that love can find no flaws in it,
for one can be faulted for the slightest thing.

The man whom this love chooses
lives happy, courtly and wise,

and the man she rejects
she destroys and utterly confounds:
for the one who wishes to revile true love
she make so daydream like a fool
he perishes because of his presumption.

Such men are false robber judges,
false husbands and perjurers,
tight-fisted false men and slanderers,
hired-tongues, church-wreckers,
and those burning whores
who consort with other women's husbands:
all these will have a reward in Hell.

Drunks and cuckolds,
false priests and abbots,
false recluses, female and male,
will be in torment there, says Marcabru;
there all false people have their space reserved,
for true love has promised this:
in that place will be the pain of the desperate.

Ah, true love, fount of virtues,
because you light up the whole world,
spare me this torment, I beg you;
prevent me from languishing there,
for everywhere I hold myself your prisoner
and your condemned criminal in everything;
by you I hope to be guided.

With this song I master my own self,
since I admonish myself more than another,
for he who wishes to accuse another

should rightfully know how to avoid
being covered in the crimes of which
he himself speaks as an accuser:
then he will be able to chastise in safety.

The 'preacher' has turned lawyer, and finally, master of eloquence:

But he is indeed among the chosen
who knows how to speak well when giving evidence,
for he can, if he wishes, regain awareness of himself.

The art of speaking well and truthfully, he declares, is a way to self-knowledge and salvation.

Our troubadour's use of the grammatical first person is not, however, limited to this kind of complex authority figure whom one might be tempted to identify as the 'real' Marcabru. Sometimes the poetic 'I' is the target of his criticism. In a famous *pastorela* he speaks as a philandering knight (xxx):

The other day, beside a hedge,
I found a common little wench . . .

I came to her across the heath.
'My pretty one,' I said, 'you lovely thing,
It pains me that you're stung by cold.'
'Sir,' said the peasant girl to me,
'thanks to God and to my nurse,
I care little if the wind dishevels me,
for I am happy about it and healthy.'

In a series of exchanges the sheperdess rebuffs his trite advances, including a misguided attempt at flattery, and sends him off with a flea in his ear:

'My pretty one, to my way of thinking
your father was a knight
who sired you in your mother,
for she was a courtly peasant woman.
The more I look at you the more it pleases me
and I brighten up with joy –
if only you were a little kind to me!'

'My lord, I see all my lineage and family
going back and reverting to the sickle and the plough,
Sir,' so said the peasant girl,
'whereas a man may act like a knight
who ought to do the same
all six days in the week.'

'My pretty one,' said I, 'a noble fairy
fashioned you when you were born:
there is in you, courtly peasant girl,
a pure and rarified beauty,
and it would be easily doubled
with just one coupling,
me on top and you beneath.'

'Sir, you have praised me so much
that I am quite annoyed about it.
Since you have exalted my reputation,'
so said the peasant girl to me,
'you shall have me as your reward
when you leave: gape, fool, gape
in your mid-day siesta!'

A la fontana del vergier (1) presents a similar first-person narrator, also an immoral knight. Here the knight attempts to take advantage of a sorrowing castellan's daughter whose lover, unlike this cowardly and selfish suitor, has left for the Second Crusade. The use of voice here is more complex than in the *pastorela*, for although the listener is led to sympathize with the girl, who is faithful to her absent lover, in her address to Jesus she is nevertheless a reminder of ecclesiastical complaints about women whose personal desires may distract men from a higher calling.

> Beside the spring she wept
> and sighed from the bottom of her heart.
> 'Jesus,' she said, 'King of the world,
> because of you there falls to me great sorrow,
> for your shame is my undoing:
> the best of all this world
> are going to serve you, since it is your will.'

A further complexity lies in her criticism of Louis, for, as we have seen, Marcabru is otherwise negative about the French king and his crusade.

> 'With you departs my beloved,
> handsome, courtly, brave and noble;
> here with me remains great distress,
> frequent longing and weeping.
> Ah, cursed be King Louis,
> who orders the call to arms and preaching
> which are the cause of this grief entering my heart!'
> (I, 15–28)

Other examples of the troubadour's play on voice include a comic dialogue between a foolish suitor and a starling – a mock messenger sent off to a woman who 'seems more cunning than a hunt-hardened old vixen' (xxv, 34–45), with a 'Marcabru' figure interspersing sardonic comments from the sidelines; a mysterious first-person cuckolder boasting of his skill at twisting the meanings of words and seducing other men's wives (XVI); and the pair of songs that gave rise to the *vida* in manuscript K (XLIII and XX), in which a minstrel who calls himself Marcabru complains of the stinginess of a lord called Audric, and Audric mocks him for thinking he could get any money out of him. It is tempting, despite the absence of evidence, to envisage dramatic performance of some or all these songs, with the involvement of actors, props or costumes.

Marcabru's enduring appeal must have depended in no small measure on his exceptional talent and his ability to entertain. Given his aggressive castigation of his social superiors, it makes sense to see him addressing primarily an audience of his peers. As Harvey has suggested, 'Perhaps he was telling them exactly what they wanted to hear?' She also insightfully suggests that Marcabru's self-references, using what was probably a stage-name, 'may have attenuated the offensiveness of some of his remarks, and helped to save him from some of the more dangerous consequences of abusing his audience'.[25]

Another remarkable troubadour and an admirer of Marcabru, Peire d'Alvernhe, shows the ambivalence of his forerunner's reception. In a song of 1157–8 supporting the Reconquista, he declares: 'I see the reputation diminishing of the one who destroys the joy of the world: he is the son of a base creature, who shows up baseness, yet for all this he does not bow his head despite being cast indifferently aside; henceforth he is found among the despised.' The final stanza reveals his identity: 'Marcabru with great rectitude composed in like manner, and all consider him a fool who are ignorant of their own nature and forget the reason they were born.'[26]

Bernart de Ventadorn, historiated initial from a *Chansonnier provençal* manuscript, 13th century.

FOUR

Bernart de Ventadorn

Bernart has been called 'one of the greatest love poets of all times'.[1] Among all troubadour poetry the captivating grace and expressivity of his lyrics, their rhythm, musicality and imagery have had the most immediate appeal to a Romantic and post-Romantic public. Love is Bernart's only subject. Veering from joy to anguish, forlorn longing to quasi-mystical ecstasy, hope to despair to serene remembrance, his songs mark the crystallization of quintessential troubadour concepts of love.

Bernart enjoyed the patronage of Viscount Eble II of Ventadour (1086–1147), 'the singer'. His songs, several preserved with music, enjoyed wide resonance in Occitania as well as northern France.[2] His contacts included Henry II of England and Eleanor of Aquitaine, and he may have gone to England with her for a time, as the *vidas* relate.[3] He also met the troubadours who, like himself, were satirized in Peire d'Alvernhe's *Cantarai d'aquestz trobadors* during the wedding celebrations in Spain in 1170 of Alfonso VIII of Castile and Eleanor of England, Henry II and Eleanor of Aquitaine's daughter.[4] That he was from the castle of Ventadorn in the Limousin, as stated by the *vidas*, is likely. Their stories about his alleged humble birth are considerably less so. They probably derive from Peire's satire, which joked that 'in his father he had a soldier good at firing with a laburnum hand bow, and his mother stoked the fire and gathered up the vine shoots', the basis for which remains a mystery.[5] Their comment that he 'knew how to sing and compose, and became courtly and educated' is to state the obvious from the texts the songbooks are recording. There is no corroboration of their statement that he eventually entered the monastery of Dalon.

The 'school of Eble'

Connected to the court of Eble II, Bernart claimed to belong to his 'school' of poetry. In one song he laments that because his lady is unresponsive he will no more be a singer (*chantaire*), or one of 'Sir Eble's school' (30, 22–3). In another (13, 55–7) he declares that 'Ventadorn will hardly be without a singer [*chantador*] any longer, for the one who is the courtliest and who knows the most about love taught me everything I know about it.' Martín de Riquer argues that the use of the preterite 'taught' (*essenhet*) shows that Bernart composed them after Eble's death in 1147, and suggests that the first stanza may allude to this as a recent occurrence:

> I certainly thought to refrain from singing until the time of the sweet gentle season; now, since no-one rejoices and I see merit and gift-giving dying out, I cannot help taking pains in the cold over a new song which will be comfort to others; and it is right, since things are going so well for me in love, that I should have better cheer for everyone.[6]

Between 1160 and 1184 the Limousin chronicler Geoffrey of Vigeois wrote that Eble loved songs of joyfulness (*alacritatis carmina dilexit*) right into his old age, and that because of his songs he was highly regarded (*valde gratiosus*) by the Count of Poitiers. Modern scholars have sought in vain to discover any of his songs.[7]

The viscount was a magnet for troubadours. Cercamon sent him his *planh* on the death of William x of Aquitaine, and Bernart Marti directed a *vers* to him 'because in him the love of a lady and a knight is *jauzida*'.[8] The word *jauzida* is interesting. Bernart Marti is very much a poet of physical love: in the same piece, for example, he declares that if his lady 'shortly consents to that which I desire, that I kiss her naked or clothed, I seek no other riches at all: I am worth much more than an emperor if I lie beside her lovely body beneath her fur mantle' (29–35). *Jauzida* can be understood as a past participle ('love is joyfully welcomed'), but equally as a noun ('love is enjoyment').[9] Troubadours delight in suggestive erotic ambivalence, and Bernart Marti seems to be hinting that Eble favours the physicality of love between knights and ladies. Such an interpretation is consonant with the earlier Marcabru's hostility to Eble's 'school': 'I will never support Sir Eble's compositions, for he upholds his foolish understanding in the face of reason. – Ai! – For I have said and say and will say that he is tight-fisted and he decries love.' Marcabru has defended *Amor* as caring for its companion, unlike *Amar*, false or bitter love, 'lust which catches fire from the wicked flame' and 'torments the senses and casts them into perdition'.[10]

Marcabru's accusation of Eble's tight-fistedness, the cardinal vice in the courtly value system,[11] may refer, perhaps ironically, to stories about rivalry between the courts of Poitiers and the Limousin over their reputation for *urbanitas* or courtliness. One anecdote concerning Eble and Guilhem ix, his nominal overlord, relates:

> Eble, brother of Pierre de Pierre-Buffière through their mother, Almode, was highly regarded because of his songs. For this reason, he was especially favoured by William, son of Guy, but they had a fierce rivalry and

each attempted to tarnish the other's reputation with the stain of inurbanity. Eble happened to arrive at Poitiers one day and enter the hall where the count was dining. Many dishes were prepared for Eble, but not immediately, so when the count finished his meal, Eble is said to have remarked, 'A count should not have had so many dishes prepared for such an insignificant viscount.' A few days later, the duke unexpectedly followed Eble as he returned home. The duke entered the court of Ventadour in a flurry with a hundred knights while Eble was dining. Eble, realizing that he was being put to the test, ordered water immediately to be brought to be poured onto their hands. Meanwhile, his retainers scoured the village and quickly brought the food they had seized to the kitchen – there was a feast of hens, geese and other fowl on that day. Eble's retainers prepared such a sumptuous banquet that many thought it seemed like the wedding day of some prince. At sunset, a certain peasant arrived drawing an ox-cart, without Eble's knowledge. He cried out like a herald: 'Come here, young bloods of the count of Poitiers, and see how wax is delivered at the lord of Ventadour's court!' So saying, he mounted his cart, took up a carpenter's axe, and broke the straps attaching his load. He broke up a barrel and countless different shapes made from the purest wax fell out. The peasant mounted his cart again, as if he considered these matters trifling, and returned to his farm at Malmont. The count, after witnessing this, praised Eble's worth and industry wherever he went. Eble promoted the peasant, giving him and his offspring the above-mentioned farm at Malmont. The sons were honoured with the belt of knighthood and are now nephews of Archambald of Solignac and of Albuin, archdeacon of Limoges.[12]

The rivalry of these courts, then, manifested itself in competitive displays of conspicuous waste and liberality, the composition of vernacular song, and concepts of love.

Fin'amor or courtly love

Bernart's view of love sets him apart from Marcabru. While Bernart may be responding to his challenge,[13] it is not out of the question that Marcabru is responding to Bernart, or that they are both involved in the same polemical discussions among troubadours and their audiences, since their datable activity overlaps by a few years at least.[14] Where Marcabru formulated his views of love in abstract, didactic terms, Bernart forcefully asserts the value of personal, sincere feeling, the hallmark of excellence in both love and poetry.

I There is little use in singing
if the song does not spring from the heart;
and the song cannot spring from the heart
4 if there is no true, heartfelt love in her.
For this reason my song is superior,
for in the joy of love I engage
my mouth and eyes and heart and mind.

II 8 May God never give me that power
not to be taken with the desire for love.
Even if I could never have anything from her,
but every day would bring me sorrow,
12 at least I should always have a good heart;
and I have much more joy from her
because I have a good heart and devote myself to her.
(15, 1–14)

Both troubadours attack foolish people for confusing true and false love and disparage venal women, but while Marcabru concedes that true love should be based on mutual desire (XXXVII, 1–14, 34), this is almost certainly within the framework of marriage. Bernart develops these points in his stress on pleasure and physicality, with not the slightest hint of marital affection.

III Foolish people blame love out of ignorance,
but this does no harm to love,
for she can in no way be diminished
unless she is vulgar love.
This is not love: this only has the name
and the appearance of it,
for it loves nothing unless it can make a profit.

IV To tell the truth, I know well enough
who gives rise to the fraud:
those women who love for money
and are mercenary traders.
I wish I were a liar and dishonest about it!
I am, shamefully, telling the truth,
and I'm sorry I'm not lying.

V In giving pleasure and in longing
is the love of two true lovers.
Nothing can be to their advantage
if their desire is not equal,
and a man is a real fool
if he reproaches her for what she wants,
and urges her to do what displeases her.

VI I have placed my good hope well.
When she gives me kind looks –

she whom I most desire and wish to see,
sincere, gentle, true and loyal,
in whom the king himself would find salvation,
beautiful and charming, with a well-formed body –
she has made me a rich man from nothing.

VII Nothing more do I love or can I fear,
nor would anything ever cause me pain,
as long as it pleased my lady,
for that day seems to me like Christmas
when with her beautiful, spiritual eyes,
she looks at me – but so lingeringly
that one day lasts a hundred.

The poet is ambiguous in verses 33–5, since it is open as to whether he is referring to love or to the woman. The one who is a 'real fool' (*fols naturaus*) is designated as masculine (*cel*), although this could cover both male and female. Bernart may be saying that one should not reproach love for one's desires, or ask anything unfitting from it; however, the sense could be that a man should not rebuke a woman for what she wants or advise her to do anything contrary to what pleases her or is fitting for her. The ambiguity is certainly intentional and leaves much unsaid.

In the *tornadas* Bernart seems to echo Marcabru's stress on his own *trobar naturau* (xxxiii, 7): 'The *vers* is true and sincere (*fis e naturaus*), and good to anyone who listens to it carefully/ understands it well (*be l'enten*), and even better for one who hopes for the joy. Bernart de Ventadorn understands it, performs it and composes it and hopes for the joy of it.' Editors have translated *fis e naturaus* in different ways, but the words are no doubt reiterating the poet's claim to sincerity. The word *enten* can mean 'understand', 'listen to' or 'pay attention to': like Guilhem ix, Bernart divides his audience into those who catch his meaning and those who do not, but he is also appealing to his audience to pay his song proper attention and not just let it flow over them (or chatter!). It is significant that he qualifies *joi* with the definite article: this is not joy in the abstract, but a particular yet unspecified joy, left to the imagination.

Bernart crystallizes the key elements of troubadour love poetry, and from this time on it makes sense to speak of a 'code' of love in its wider sense of a language of initiates. The courtly *canso* as a whole deploys a range of characteristic *topoi* or commonplace ideas, phrases, motifs and stylistic devices that form part of such a code. These include the spring opening; professions of love, constancy, timidity, sincerity and discretion; apostrophes to Love; evocations of the *domna* and the *lauzengiers* (tale-telling slanderers interfering with love); comparisons of the lover with famous lovers such as Tristan; representations of the *domna* as a feudal overlord whose submissive lover serves her as her quasi-vassal and worshipper; discussions of the nature of love and courtly virtues; and key concepts such as joy, youth, courtliness, generosity, merit, worth, moderation and more.[15] With a few exceptions troubadours henceforth defend *fin'amor* as a source of moral goodness and worth, some emphasizing the virtuous qualities of the individual, others the social benefits of the court.[16]

Artistry and the *trobar leu*

Bernart's style is generally considered to belong to the *trobar leu*, the clear, light, accessible style. This is deceptive. His style may be uncomplicated by veiled meanings or recondite vocabulary, but it is far from simple. Its emotional intensity lies not only in its wealth of images and vocabulary of joy and suffering but in an intricate, virtually untranslatable weaving of sound and wordplay. *Can vei la lauzeta mover* (43) is a quintessential

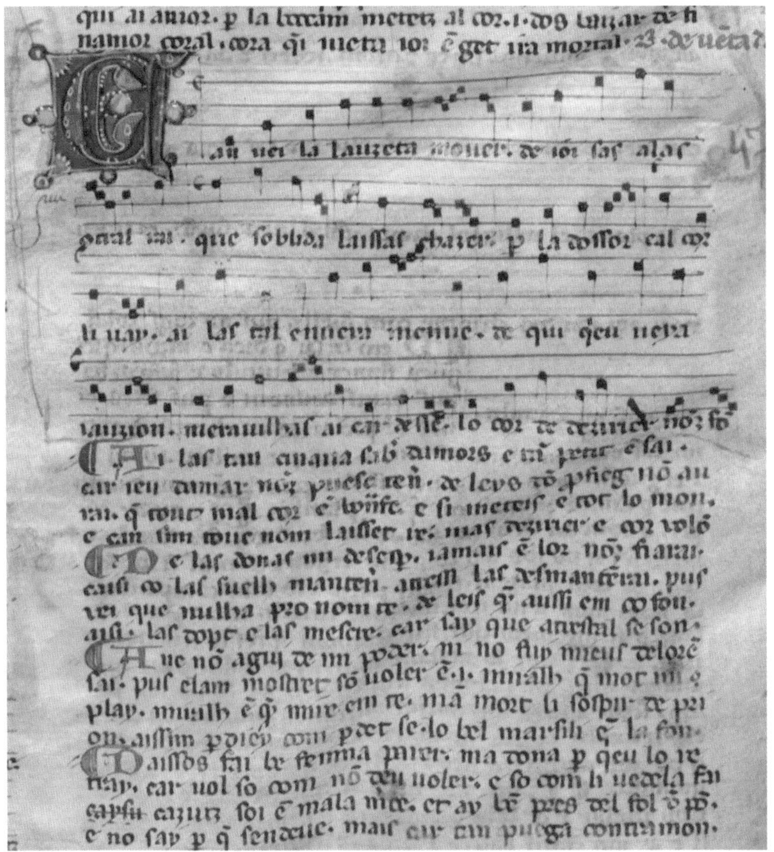

Can vei la lauzeta mover, musical notation from a *Chansonnier provençal* manuscript, 14th century.

example of this. Widely anthologized and set to music, it epitomizes the musicality of his words and his ability to conjure deep and powerful feelings.

I Can vei la lauzeta mover
de joi sas alas contral rai
Que s'oblid'e.s laissa chazer
4 per la dousor c'al cor li vai,
ai, tan grans enveyea m'en ve

de cui qu'eu veya jauzion,
meravilhas ai, car desse
lo cor de dezirer no.m fon.

II Ai! las, tan cuidava saber
d'amor e tan petit en sai,
car eu d'amar no'm posc tener
celeis don ja pro non aurai.
Tout m'a mo cor e tout m'a me
e se mezeis e tot lo mon,
e can se.m tolc, no.m laisset re
mas dezirer e cor volon.

III Anc non agui de me poder
ni no fui meus de l'or' en sai
Que.m laisset en sos olhs vezer
en un miralh que mout me plai.
Miralhs, pus me mirei en te,
m'an mort li sospir de preon
c'aissi.m perdei com perdet se
lo bels Narcisus en la fon.

IV De la domnas me dezesper.
Ja mais en lor no.m fiarai,
c'aissi com las solh chaptener,
enaissi las deschaptenrai.
Pois vei c'una pro no m'en te
va leis que.m destrui e.m confon,
totas las dopt' e las mescre,
car be sai c'atretals se son.

V D'aisso fa be femna parer
ma domna, per que.lh o retrai,

car no vol so c'om deu voler
e so c'om li deveda fai.
Chazutz sui en mala merce
et ai be faih co.l fols en pon,
e no sai per que m'esdeve
mas car trop puyai contra mon.

VI Merces es perduda per ver,
et eu non o saubi anc mai,
car cilh qui plus en degr'aver
no.n a ges, et on la querrai?
A, can mal sembla, qui la ve,
qued aquest chaitiu deziron
que ja ses leis non aura be
laisse morir, que no l'aon.

VII Pus ab midons no.m pot valer
precs ni merces ni.l dreihz qu'eu ai,
ni a leis no ven a plazer
qu'eu l'am, ja mais no.lh o dirai.
Aissi.m part de leis e.m recre.
Mort m'a e per mort li respon,
e vau m'en pus ilh no.m rete,
chaitius, en issilh, no sai on.

VIII Tristans, ges no.n auretz de me,
qu'eu m'en vau, chaitius, no sai on.
De chantar me gic e.m recre,
e de joi e d'amor m'escon.

I. When I see the lark beat its wings for joy against the sunlight, forget itself and plummet down for the sweetness than enters its heart, ah! such great envy/longing comes to me from those I see filled with joy that I marvel my heart does not instantly melt from desire.

II. Alas! so much I thought to know of love, and so little do I know of it, for I cannot keep from loving her in whom I never shall find favour. She has stolen my heart, and stolen me from myself, and herself, and the whole world; and when she robbed me of myself she left me nothing but desire and a yearning heart.

III. Never did I have power over myself, nor was I my own, from the moment she let me see into her eyes, in a mirror that pleases me greatly. Mirror, since I saw myself in/gazed on you, sighs from the depths have been my death. I have lost myself just as the fair Narcissus lost himself in the fountain.

IV. I despair of ladies. I shall have no further faith in them. Just as I used to defend them, so I shall deprecate them. Since I see that not one of them supports me against the one who ruins and confounds me, I doubt and disbelieve them all, for well I know they are all alike.

V. In this my lady acts like a woman, which is why I reproach her; she does not want what one ought to want, and what one forbids her to do, she does. I have fallen into ill-favour, and I have acted like the fool on the bridge; and I do not know why this has happened to me except that I tried to climb too high.

VI. Mercy is lost, in truth, and never have I known it yet; for the one who most should have it has none at all, and where shall I seek it? Ah! how bad it must seem to anyone who looks at her that she is allowing this wretched prisoner of desire, who will never have anything good without her, to die without lifting a hand to help him.

VII. Since neither prayers nor pity nor the rights I have are of any avail with my lady, nor does it please her that I love her, I shall no longer tell her of it. Thus I part from her and abandon her service/confess myself defeated. She has been the death of me, and I answer her with death, and go away, since she does not retain me in her service, wretched, exiled, I know not where.

VIII. Tristan, you will have no more from me, for I am going away, wretched, I know not where. I forsake and renounce singing, and hide from joy and love.

The song begins with a nature opening, a common device generally deployed to evoke or contrast with the poet's mood, or to offer a pretext for singing. Bernart's limpid image of the lark hovering in ecstasy against the sun and plummeting to the ground in self-forgetfulness is far from commonplace or simple. The poet is both distant from the lark and identified with it. Distant, he gazes on this delicate embodiment of others' joy, and is filled with *enveia* – a word meaning both envy and desire – at the sight of those who are joyous and satisfied (*jauzion*). At the same time he identifies with the lark in its soaring aspiration to the sublime, whose unbearable sweetness leads to self-forgetfulness and a sudden fall to earth – a fall which for the poet brings the pain of separation from others, the beloved, and his own sense of self. Stanza II, blending introspection and lament, reinforces the sense of loss, blaming the adored but dangerous *domna* for robbing him of himself, herself and his anchorage in the world. It also makes a fleeting, ironic and perhaps gently playful nod to

Bernart's authority in matters of love (9–10), evoking his relationship to the social world of his audience. After all, he stands before them, performing.

Intricate sound effects intensify ideas of seeing, moving and feeling (***vei***, *mo**ver***, *en**ve**ya*, ***ve**ya*, ***ve***), of the heart and its sweetness (*douss**or***, *c**or***, *c**or***). The sound of lament *ai*, anticipated in the rhymes from the beginning (*r**ai***, *v**ai***, *meravilhas **ai***), leads into the heartfelt cry **Ai**! *las* and reverberates throughout the song in every second and fourth line of the full stanzas. The melody as shown in manuscript R partly follows the movement of the lark and the poet's emotions in stanza I, rising like the lark to a high note on *alas* (wings), hovering until beginning to fall on *s'oblida* (forgets itself) and on down to *chazer* (fall), then developing independently of the words' content, until emphasizing the final word of this and each stanza with a falling cadence and lingering ornament.[17]

In stanza III the poet compares himself with Narcissus, who in Ovid's *Metamorphoses* fell in love with his own reflection in a pool and died, languishing for an impossible love. What does Bernart see in the mirror of his lady's eyes? Most have thought it is his own reflection, 'his own image perfected by every courtly grace and virtue', or, in mystical, theological terms, an image of him which the lady, 'a sort of Beatrice of multiple identities, woman, *sophia*, hypostasis of some sapiential knowledge', allows him to see for just a brief moment.[18] The distinguished medieval scholar Sarah Kay has pointed out, however, that *me mirei en* (v. 21) does not necessarily mean 'saw myself reflected in', but can also mean 'gazed on, considered', and that other examples of the Narcissus myth in medieval literature, together with scientific theories of vision of that time, show that 'mediaeval man looking into a mirror would expect to see something other than himself in it.'[19] The mirror in *Can vei la lauzeta*, she argues, 'acts as a source of enlightenment since it is immediately after looking into it that Bernart comprehends the reality of his position'; the metaphor serves to communicate 'a valuable insight into a hidden truth'. She also argues that what the poet sees here emerges from the structure of the poem, the mirror being a structural device in both this stanza and the song as a whole. Stanza III is built 'round two standard motifs: praise of the lady (here specifically her eyes) and the extremity of the lover's suffering':

> The play *miralh/mirei* sets up a verbal reflection which reinforces the semantic content of the image, and is in turn reinforced by other similar reflections or repetitions. In this stanza we have *miralh–miralhs*, and also *perdet-perdei*, itself set in a chiasmic structure which formally mimics the reflecting action of a mirror and so emphasizes the parallel between the fates of Narcissus and the lover. In other words, the mirror is present not only as a metaphor for the lady's eyes but as a formal device throughout the stanza.[20]

Meanwhile verbal repetitions and morphological play pervade the song as a whole,

> most evident in the echoing *tornada* (57–60) which reproduces in slightly altered form the material of lines 55–56. The fatal power of the mirror's reflection is brought out formally as well as explicitly in line 54 by the repetition of *mort*: 'mort m'a, e per mort li respon'.[21]

Whatever their 'original' order,[22] stanzas IV and V in this edition develop the *domna*'s role in misogynistic, even playful ways. They set the lover in the ordinary, refractory world. The *domna* drops her elevated status as an idealized figure of command, and becomes a mere *femna* or 'woman', one among many, and for the Middle Ages a stereotypically unreliable object of disparagement and mistrust. The 'fool on the bridge' echoes and anticipates ideas of falling and trying to climb too high (vv. 3, 37, 40). The medieval *Proverbe au vilain*, stating that 'the wise man does not fall on the bridge,' glosses 'because he dismounts': no doubt to avoid falling not just to the ground but down to the watery depths below, like Narcissus perhaps, but with less dignity and more self-deprecation.

The whole *canso*, like countless others in the troubadour corpus, forms an appeal to the lady's pity. Stanza VI expresses this most directly, developing the motif in stanza VII in quasi-feudal terms that present the *domna* – otherwise addressed as the masculinized *midons* (49, 'my lord') – as overlord. The metaphors are rhetorical, suggestive rather than logical. Although the poet speaks of her duties (35–6, 43) and his rights (50), he says himself that she does not retain him in her service (*rete*, 55), and there is nothing in the poem to show that she ever has: if anything she has behaved like a robber (13–15) rather than a suzerain. The phrase *.m recre* (53) is ambiguous: continuing with the feudal metaphor it can be understood as 'I abandon her service,' but it also means 'I confess myself defeated,' as in battle. Kay's observation nevertheless brings out the social aspect of his loss:

> This evocation of the contractual relationship between overlord and vassal gives greater meaning to Bernart's final departure into exile: he experiences not only self-loss and loss of the lady, but also exclusion from the whole network of reciprocal relationships which regulates and gives meaning to courtly society, whether to feudalism itself or to its metaphorical extension to the art of love.[23]

The pseudonym or *senhal* in the *tornada* is enigmatic. Stories of Tristan, the famous lover exiled from society and fated to die for his love of the king Mark's wife Yseut, abound in medieval literature, and the name imbues the lines with tragedy. But who is meant by it? Some have thought it stands for the poet's *domna*. Yet even if a masculine pseudonym for a woman addressee is not unknown, why should the unmoved *domna* acquire a name so redolent of sadness? It is more likely to be a *senhal* for a man who may, as it has been argued, be the troubadour Raimbaut d'Aurenga. If so, and if it conjures a sense of social loss, it simultaneously reaffirms a relationship. If he addresses a friend, even if in farewell, surely the song will be sent to him.

Versification, rhetoric and music

The artistry of Bernart's versification, generally unobtrusive though occasionally more ostentatiously virtuoso, has been well described by modern commentators.[24] *Tant ai mo cor ple de joya* (44) is an example of his more elaborate interweaving of rhyme-words. Composed entirely of feminine rhymes, and a mixture of line lengths, it begins,

Tant ai mo cor ple de joya
    tot me desnatura.
Flor blancha, vermelh' e groya
    me par la frejura,
c'ab lo ven et ab la ploya
    me creis l'aventura,
per que mos pretz mont' e poya
    e mos chans melhura.
  Tan ai al cor d'amor,
  de joi e de doussor,
per que.l gels me sembla flor
    e la neus verdura.

> I have my heart so full of joy, everything is metamorphosed for me. The cold seems to me a white, scarlet and yellow flower, for my fortune grows with the wind and the rain, so my merit climbs and rises and my song improves. I have so much joy in my heart, so much joy and sweetness, that the frost seems to me like a flower, and the snow, greenery.

The rhyme scheme follows the pattern *a b a b a b a b* C *c c b*, where the C rhyme-word, *amor,* is stable. Frank represents this as *a: oja, ura, iza, ansa, onda, aire; b: ura, iza, anza, onda, aire, ire; c: or, with v. 8 'amor'*. This means on a practical level that Bernart needs to find up to eight words ending in the same rhyme and fit them to short lines of seven, six and five syllables. In addition, he picks up the last line of each stanza in the first rhyme of the next one, so the initial *b* rhyme becomes the new *a* one, and a new *b* rhyme is introduced, in a sort of 'spiral progression'.[25] All this takes place within a perfectly coherent structure, grammatically, thematically and tonally, containing some of the loveliest lines of troubadour poetry: 'Ai Deus, car no sui ironda/ que voles per l'aire/ e vengues de noih prionda/ lai dins so repaire (51–4)? (Ah God, would that I were a swallow that might fly through the air, and come in the dead of night right into her room!)

As well as versification, the tools of Bernart's trade include many traditional rhetorical devices. Anna Ferrari highlights enjambements, alliteration, *chiasmus*, *accumulatio*, *sententiae*, an immense variety of exordial topoi relating to the psychology of the lover, the use of verb tenses and moods, the creation of movement, circularity and undulation.[26] Nichols brings out Bernart's subtle use of time: suspended in the lingering gaze of his *domna* as if Christmas Day lasts a hundred ordinary days;[27] or dragged out when no favour from her is forthcoming: 'Time goes, and comes, and turns, through days, through months and through years, and I, alas, know not what to say, for my desire is always one. Always it is one and changeless, for I want and always wanted one from whom I never did have joy' (30, 1–4).

Nineteen of Bernart's 45 songs are preserved with musical notation: a rich proportion in comparison with that of the other great troubadours of his generation. Carapezza comments that there may be historical reasons for this, but that it seems more likely to stem from the intrinsic quality of his music. Carapezza's analysis of a small selection of four pieces shows differentiation between their forms and musical types. *Can vei la flor* (42) and *Lancan folhan bosc e jarric* (24) he describes as characterized by the continuous, homogeneous development of the melodic line and by a contemplative and almost mystical movement of the singing. This contrasts with *En cossirer et en esmai* (17) and *Lancan vei la folha* (25), where structural repetitions of simple, sparsely ornamented phrases make it easy to sing and remember, and the notation suggests a definite rhythm and the influence of folkloric tradition and instrumental forms; the forms of *Lancan vei la folha* in particular seem more like those designed for the *dansa* than for the *canso*, and may perhaps have been designed to be choreographed.[28] *Can vei la flor*, based wholly on decasyllables, was to be the pre-eminent model for the *canso* in the last quarter of the twelfth century and played an essential role in the spread of the Occitan lyric in Europe.

Whether or not Bernart sings of his own feelings, which is unknowable, sincerity is his professional pitch.[29] This in no way detracts from his power to move. A supreme artist, he veils his art with an illusion of spontaneity.

FIVE

The *Trobairitz*

We know of approximately twenty named *trobairitz* or women troubadours from the twelfth and thirteenth centuries: a considerable number in comparison with the contemporary vernacular writers of France or Anglo-Norman England. Their surviving corpus is nonetheless tiny in comparison with the 2,500 or so texts by men: if an explicit reference in a poem to the act of composition carried out by the feminine lyric 'I' makes plausible the hypothesis of female authorship,[1] there may be around twenty-five or thirty such texts: a *canso*, two *sirventes*, a *planh*, an indeterminate number of *tensos*, two *partimens*, seven exchanges of *coblas*, two *dansas* and *baladas*, perhaps an *alba*, and a poetic letter.[2] Their manuscript transmission is fragile: nineteen of their pieces only appear in a single songbook. Other *trobairitz* may be concealed among anonymous songs in a feminine first-person voice, or else among dialogues involving an unnamed *domna* and a male troubadour, named or not. Many such texts may have been entirely male authored, though it is perverse simply to make this assumption, for how often has male authorship itself been questioned? Occasionally we learn of a *trobairitz* without surviving songs, such as Caudairenga, said in a *razo* of Raimon de Miraval to be good at composing *coblas* and *dansas*.[3]

Almost all the named *trobairitz* are aristocrats, or appear to be. A minority of Occitan noblewomen of the twelfth and thirteenth centuries enjoyed considerable political and economic power in comparison with women of later centuries.[4] They collaborated in the game of courtly love, patronized troubadour poetry, composed poetry themselves and engaged in entertaining and flirtatious discourse with men as part of the *solatz*, or congenial social environment of the courts, celebrated by the troubadours.

Cansos

Trobairitz composing *cansos* include Azalais de Porcairagues, Castelloza, Clara d'Anduza, the Comtessa de Dia, Tibors de Sarenom and perhaps Bieiris de Romans.[5] They write mainly within the conventions of the male *canso*, which gives rise to some interesting difficulties: how can the *domna* write of her erotic longings and disappointments when the male troubadour's song generally typecasts her as the haughty, glacial, demanding though unvoiced figure he serves? How can the *trobairitz* reveal her identity by the very fact of singing in her own name, when convention requires secrecy? How can she protect her reputation, when it is all too easy to call a woman a slut?

The *trobairitz* can be surprisingly candid in expressing their desires – assuming, of course, that they are speaking in their own voice. The seventeenth century saw the Comtessa de Dia as a scarlet woman, and Alfred Jeanroy in the early twentieth was shocked at their immodesty. Azalais de Porcairagues evokes an erotic situation which led René Nelli to construct a whole theory of courtly love around a ritual *asag* or carnal 'test':[6] 'Fair love, I have pledged to be always well disposed towards you, courtly and welcoming, provided you do not ask me to go too far. We shall soon come to the test of this, for I shall put myself at your mercy; you have promised me faithfully that you will not ask me to do anything wrong.'[7] Yet more candid is the Comtessa de Dia:

> I would like to hold my knight naked in my arms one evening, for he would be overjoyed if I only served him as a pillow. I have been more enamoured of him than Floris was of Blancheflor, and I grant him my heart and my love, my mind, my eyes and my life. Fair friend, charming and kind, when shall I hold you in my power? If only I could lie with you one evening and give you a loving kiss! Know that I should dearly love to hold you in the place of husband, provided that you promised me to do everything I wish.[8]

One explanation for this apparent frankness is that the *trobairitz* draw on a second, popularizing tradition of 'women's songs', where the female speaker 'typically sings of her longings, her physical charms and desires, [and] falls into despair without her lover to whom she offers total submission', as in the following anonymous piece:[9]

I am pretty, so I'm much troubled
by my husband whom I neither want nor desire.
And I'll tell you why I'm troubled:
I am pretty . . .
it's because I'm a petite, very young girl,
I am pretty . . .
and I ought to have a husband who would make me joyful,
with whom I could play and laugh all the time.
I am pretty . . .

May God never save me if I am in love with him;
I am pretty . . .
I have absolutely no desire to love him!
I am pretty . . .
Instead, when I see him I feel such shame

that I beg death to come and kill him on the spot.
I am pretty . . .

And I'll tell you what I have decided:
I am pretty . . .
since my lover has loved me for so long
I am pretty . . .
now my love will be entirely at his disposal
I am pretty . . .[10]

Whatever the explanation, there is in fact no evidence that contemporaries criticized the women composers of *cansos*, and thirteenth- and fourteenth-century illuminators show only respect for their nobility and role in courtly life.[11]

In her one surviving song Azalais seems untroubled by such issues. A mixture of different elements, perhaps due to the heterogeneous nature of the manuscript transmission, it combines a lament for the troubadour Raimbaut d'Aurenga's death in 1173 with comments on the nature of her love and of love in general. The latter seem to refer to a debate, live in around 1170, over the difference of social status between lover and beloved, involving the troubadours Guilhem de Sant-Leidier, Raimbaut himself, Guiraut de Borneil and King Alfonso II of Aragon: 'A lady very badly misplaces her love when she engages with a man who is too powerful, higher than a vavassor [literally 'vassal of a vassal'], and if she does, she acts foolishly. In Velay they say that love does not go with power, and a lady who is seen to do so I consider dishonoured' (vv. 17–24).[12]

From Portiragnes near Béziers (Hérault), and designated in her *vida* with the honorific *Na* or 'Lady', Azalais was well integrated into the courtly life of the region. She sends the song to the viscountess Ermengard of Narbonne, a well-known patron of troubadours, and Raimbaut dedicated twelve of his *cansos* to

Azalais de Porcairagues, historiated initial from a *Chansonnier provençal* manuscript, 13th century.

her, calling her *Joglar*. Her winter opening and initial rhyme-sounds (*-ut*, *-aigna*) are a poetic tribute to him.[13]

> Now we have come to the cold time,
> and the ice and the snow and the mud,
> and the little birds are mute,
> for none of them attempts to sing;
> and the boughs in the hedges are bare,
> with no blossom or leaf sprouting,
> nor the nightingale calling
> that wakes me there in May. (1–8)

Her concluding, elegiac stanza reinforces a sense of community, and still resonates today with those familiar with Orange:

> To God I commend Belesgar
> along with the city of Orange,
> and Glorieta and the castle,
> and the lord of Provence

and all my well-wishers there,
and the arch where the famous deeds are represented.
I have lost the one who has my life,
and I shall always sorrow for it. (41–8)

The arch still stands, a link to Provence's Roman and medieval past.

Azalais gives an impression of self-confidence in love, her place in society and her words; if words partly fail her, as she says, it is because of her sorrowful loss of a dear friend (13–16) and not for any other reason. But as Sarah Kay has observed, the *cansos* of other *trobairitz* betray a sense of insecurity arising from the constraints of the genre. The unidentified Na Castelloza reverses its traditional male-female roles. By placing herself in the role of the man humbly requesting, she rejects the role of

Triumphal arch at Orange, southeast France, built between 27 BC and AD 14 (?).

Na Castelloza, historiated initial from *Recueil des poésies des troubadours*, 13th century.

Comtessa de Dia, historiated initial from *Recueil des poésies des troubadours*, 13th century.

the haughty lady, adopts a subordinate stance and draws on stereotypes of the passionate women generally excluded from the *canso* but found in popularizing genres.[14] As a submissive woman pleading with a man she expresses the awkwardness of her position, since ‘everyone says it is most unseemly for a lady to beg a knight on her own behalf or make long speeches to him’ (29, 8–20); ‘I shall have set a truly bad example to other women in love, for it is a man who usually sends a message and well-chosen and selected words’ (31, 21–4).

While the unidentified Comtessa de Dia adopts a different strategy by accepting the role of the *domna*, this too can be a source of anxiety.[15] Her best-known song, *A chantar m’er de so q’ieu no volria*, is found in many medieval manuscripts, modern anthologies and musical recordings, and is the only *trobairitz* song for which a melody survives.[16] It presents a female speaker lamenting her dismissive treatment by her lover, despite her possessing all the courtly *domna*’s desirable qualities: ‘Nothing finds grace with him: neither my mercy nor courtliness, nor my beauty, my reputation or wisdom. I am deceived and betrayed just as I should be if I were wholly without charm . . . I ought to be able to count on my reputation and my rank, my beauty and even more my true heart.’[17]

However, she is well able to ‘try on a wide variety of self-images’:[18]

Ab joi et ab joven m’apais
  e jois e jovens m’apaia
car mos amics es lo plus gais
  e per qu’ieu sui coindet’e gaia;
  e pois eu li sui veraia
be.is taing q’el me sia verais,
c’anc de lui amar no m’estrais
  ni ai cor que m’en estraia.[19] (46.1, 1–8)

I satisfy myself with joy and youth,
and joy and youth make me satisfied,
for my lover is the merriest,
which is why I am gracious and merry;
and since I am true to him,
it is proper that he should be true to me,
for I never draw back from loving him,
nor wish to draw back from this.

The song is constructed on grammatically derived rhymes, each pair of lines alternating with the masculine and feminine versions of the same rhyme word. This both shows off the *trobairitz*'s confident (if not entirely pure)[20] poetic technique and highlights the concepts and feelings conveyed by the repeated rhyme-words: initially satisfaction, gaiety, sincerity and commitment. The rhyme scheme also has the effect of intertwining the masculine and feminine elements of the song, thus mirroring the reciprocity and intimacy of the relationship sought:

He pleases me greatly, for I know he is the worthiest,
he whom I most desire to have me.
To the one who first drew him to me
I pray God to bring great joy,
and if anyone reproaches him for this,
he should pay no heed to him, but only to any reproach
  of mine,
for people often raise the cane
with which they cane themselves. (9–16)

Kay rightly draws attention to the Comtessa's 'admission of the ideologically exposed position of a woman troubadour, an admission which becomes explicit in her carefully lodged appeal for social approval or her declaration' that:[21]

a lady who aspires to great distinction
ought to place her affection
in a knight of merit and valour,
once she recognises his worth,
so that she dares to love openly;
and once a lady loves openly,
worthy, gracious people afterwards
will say only gracious things about it.

I have chosen an excellent, noble man
through whom merit improves and becomes nobler:
generous, courtly and discriminating,
where there is sense and discrimination.
I beg him to trust in me,
and for no-one to make him trust
that I commit any fault towards him,
as long as I find no fault in him. (17–32)

At the same time, it is remarkable that in defiance of any secrecy convention, she advocates daring to love openly, and makes it explicit that fault can be found in either partner.

Sirventes

The *sirventes*, a genre involving invective and strong moral and political opinions, presents women troubadours with a different issue: just how opinionated are they allowed to be?

Of the three *sirventes* in Rieger's edition, only one is ascribed to a named *trobairitz*. Gormonda de Montpellier's piece (44) is a violent invective in defence of Rome during the Albigensian wars: a blow-by-blow riposte to Guilhem Figueira's well-known *sirventes* against Rome and the clergy. Europe as a whole and the Midi in particular were undergoing a period of intense turbulence. Pope Gregory IX and Emperor Frederick II, who was planning to go on crusade in the East, were at violent loggerheads, while Count Raymond VII of Toulouse was struggling to recover the lands he had lost during the Albigensian Crusade. His supporters were hoping that Frederick could be persuaded to intervene against the French, and their hatred of the clergy naturally merged with the anticlerical stance of the emperor's own supporters (known as Ghibellines). Troubadours generally voiced outrage at what they saw as a perversion of the true purpose of crusading, and contrasted the call of the Holy Land with the 'false crusade' of the French against Toulouse.

Guilhem Figueira was the most violently outspoken of the Occitan Ghibelline poets. His long, hammering invective against Rome was widely known and reported in Inquisitorial proceedings.[22] It attacks a power-hungry papacy both for its crusade against Christians and for its attempts to sabotage the emperor's rightful crusade to the Holy Land:

> Rome, without cause you have killed many people, and I hate the twisting path you follow, Rome, because you close the door to salvation. Anyone who follows in your footsteps has a bad helmsman, in both summer and winter, because the Devil bears him off to the fire of Hell . . . Rome, it is easy to see what evil should be said of you, since you make martyrs of Christians so that you can jeer at them. But in what book do you find it written, Rome, that Christians should be killed? . . . Rome, from the bile you keep in your throat comes the liquor which causes the wicked man to die and to choke from the heart's sweetness. So the wise man trembles when he recognises and sees the deadly venom and where it comes from: Rome, your breast is full of it, and it oozes from your heart . . . You have the face of a lamb with an innocent look,

> [but] inside [you are] a ravening wolf, a crowned serpent sired by a viper, which is why the Devil looks after you like one of his close friends.[23]

Gormonda retaliates with the rhetoric of praise and blame, coupled with violent threats (46). Rome, she proclaims, is the source of all perfection and salvation; Guillem is an 'ignorant fraud', a 'rabid madman who broadcasts so many false words', and her grim, vengeful peroration invokes God's assistance in making him 'die under the same law and with the same punishment by which a heretic dies'. Far from supporting Frederick's crusading efforts in the East, she declares that those seeking salvation 'should at once take the cross in order to crush and wreck the false heretics', in other words in the Midi.

> None of you should be surprised if I wage war on an ignorant fraud who tries his utmost to bury all good courtly actions, and persecutes and imprisons them. He presumes great audacity in speaking ill of Rome, which is the leader and guide of all those who on earth have virtuous souls. In Rome all good things are brought to perfection, and anyone who takes these away from her has lost his senses, because he is deceiving himself; he will be buried for it and lose his presumptuousness. God hear my prayer: may those sharp-beaked slanderers against the Roman faith, young and old, fall from the weighing scales [into Hell]. Rome, I regard the people who load their flesh and bones with base vices as stupid, uncouth, blind and sightless; because of this they fall into the pit where stinking evil fire is prepared for them, so they are never released from the burden of their sins . . . Rome, may the great King who is Lord of righteousness bring great misfortune upon the false people of Toulouse, for

> all outrageously flout His commands, and each of them conceals this, and they destabilise this world; and I shall not consider count Raymond good if he seeks their support any more . . . Rome, may the Glorious One who pardoned the Magdalene, and from Whom we hope for a good gift, make the rabid madman who broadcasts so many false words, and his treasure, and his wicked heart, die under the same law and with the same punishment by which a heretic dies.

Gormonda is thought to have composed her *sirventes* in Montpellier, a town that remained staunchly orthodox during the Albigensian Crusade and was a centre of Catholic preaching against heresy.[24] Outspoken she certainly is; but she has male orthodoxy on her side.

The manuscripts ascribe Rieger's two other *sirventes* to male authors. One is a complaint by a woman about a sumptuary law (44) which she calls on James I of Aragon and the pope to abolish, criticizing the mendicant orders for trying to enforce their ideal of poverty by imposing sobriety and modesty in dress.

> With grievous thoughts and in grievous sorrow and in dreadful torment I lament and sigh. When I look at myself my heart almost breaks, and my eyes turn away as I see my richly decorated clothes finely trimmed with gold interwoven with silver, and gaze at my diadem. I wish the pope of Rome would have those who make us cut off our trimmings burned alive . . .

> Sir gilders and gold- and silversmiths, ladies and young girls belonging to their guild, let us send a messenger to the pope that he may excommunicate counsellors and advisers; the minor friars are greatly to blame for all this;

> and the preachers and those who dispense penances are full of ill-will over it, as are the other regular orders who are accustomed to preach about it . . .
>
> I am very anxious about my white shirt which was richly sewn with silk, yellow and scarlet and black too, white and blue, with gold and with silver. Unhappy me! I dare not wear it! . . . Sirs, make me a hairshirt for I like wearing that just as much as clothes without embroidery.

The single manuscript ascribes this piece, which it names as a *sirventesca*, to the otherwise unknown P. Basc. Paolo Di Luca has argued that it is a parody of an attack by Bernart Sicart de Marvejols on the French and the clergy during the French occupation of the south of modern-day France during the Albigensian Crusade.[25] The sentiment driving the actions and words of the woman is vanity, he argues, the feminine lyric, whether genetic or textual, being used to re-elaborate thematic elements of the model from a different, slyly misogynistic angle. He notes that the *sirventesca* contains elements of spontaneity and subjectivity typical of popularizing genres: a deliberate irony given that it imitates an elevated model. The term *sirventesca* would have been created to designate a *sirventes* with a feminine voice.

The attribution of the third *sirventes* (45) to the well-known troubadour Raimon Jordan has been decisively refuted,[26] and there is no reason to doubt its female authorship. We have met it before, in the context of Marcabru, whom the author of this song accuses of vilifying women. The speaker asserts her right to defend her sisters against misogynistic troubadours:

> I cannot help but speak my opinion
> concerning something that is making me very upset.
> This will be very displeasing and heavy for me to express,

for I say that those early troubadours
of the past are profoundly sinful.
They have imbued the world with false belief
by speaking ill of women in public;
and all those who hear this believe it to be true,
and they agree that it is very likely to be so –
and this is how they have led the world into error.
(1–10)

There is a broad tradition of medieval misogynistic writing and a lesser one of defending women.[27] This Occitan piece not only ventures to attack the authority of past troubadours, but to this end uses strong language commonly applied to heresy (*error, erransa*). The *trobairitz* finds it necessary to defend herself for expressing her opinion in public, here and elsewhere, but does so robustly:

It should be no surprise to anyone
if I speak like this or wish to demonstrate elsewhere
that every man should defend/speak to [*razonar*] his
brother,
and every woman her sister,
for Adam was our first father
and we have the Lord God as our authority.
If I therefore choose to defend/speak [*far razonamen*]
to ladies, do not blame me for anything;
for one lady ought to honour/speak to another [*far onransa,*
far razonansa],
and this is why I have expressed my opinion. (31–40)

The single manuscript contains the word *razonanza* in verse 39 and *honransa* is an emendation to fit the scansion, accepted in Rieger's edition, though in her note she indicates scholars' doubts about this. The words based on *razonar* (v. 32 and *razonamen* v. 37) can indicate both speaking to and defending someone. Whichever is the more appropriate interpretation, it would seem that the poet is defending her right to speak out but that, to deflect criticism, emphasizes that this is essentially a matter between women. Given that she has already blamed male authorities this will hardly wash – but someone at least saw fit to preserve her words.

Debates

Debate songs seem to have been a normal pastime for women, at least in the late thirteenth-century Catalan environment of Amanieu de Sescas, who reminds a noble girl to keep them decent: 'If you want to pass the time agreeably with *jocx partitz* [*partimens*], don't make them vulgar, but compose pleasing, courtly ones.'[28] If all the *tensos*, *partimens* and exchanges of *coblas* in Rieger's collection are included, debates outnumber all the other *trobairitz* genres, though there is considerable uncertainly because of the difficulty of identifying which of the unnamed *domnas* in question are actual authors. Even so, the very fact of inventing a female partner would seem to confirm the customary nature of the practice. Named female participants in dialogue pieces include Alaisina, Alamanda, Almuc de Castelnau, Carenza, the Comtessa de Proensa, Felipa (d'Anduza or de Dia), Guillelma de Rosers, Isabella, Iseut de Capion, Maria de Ventadorn, Yselda and the mysteriously designated (and no doubt fictive) Domna H. Almost all were aristocratic, some being figures of considerable power and prestige. The Comtessa de Proensa, otherwise known as Garsenda de Sabran or Garsenda de Forcalquier, was one of the most powerful women in Occitan history. Countess of both Forcalquier and Provence, she was married to Count Alfonso II of Provence, son of King Alfonso II of Aragon,[29] and

Garsenda de Forcalquier as she appears on her seal, from a drawing by Louis Blancard, 1860.

seems to have made the court in Aix-en-Provence a cultural centre and meeting place for troubadours. According to his *vida*, Elias de Barjols composed his *cansos* about her for as long as she lived.[30] A few of her lines have survived, from an exchange of *coblas* with Gui de Cavaillon (5).

Alaisina, Yselda and Carenza

An intriguing exchange apparently involving two female speakers and a silent third discuss the relative attractions of marriage and virginity:

> Fair, lovely Lady Carenza,
> give some counsel to us two sisters.
> Since you best know how to choose the better side,
> in the light of your experience do you advise me
> to take a husband, in your judgement?
> Or shall I remain a virgin? I find this attractive,
> for childbearing doesn't appeal to me;
> yet it seems very wretched not to have a husband.

Lady Alaisina and Yselda, I see that you are well
brought up,
and that you have merit and beauty, youth, a fresh
complexion,
courtliness and worth above all other well-educated ladies;
so I advise you, in order to produce good seed,
to take a husband crowned with wisdom,
through whom you will make fruit of a glorious son.
Honoured is the virgin of such a spouse!

Lady Carenza, I like the idea of taking a husband,
but I think it must be a great penance to make babies,
for your breasts sag right down
to your flabby, wrinkled, disgusting belly.

Lady Alaisina and Yselda, keep me in your remembrance;
when you go into the shadow of his protection,
pray to the Glorious One
that at our parting he will keep me close to you.[31]

The textual transmission is problematic and it has given rise to numerous interpretations, mystical and otherwise, but Di Luca has convincingly shown it to be a parody of two other poems of the same form concerning the entry of two real women into a convent. In these other poems the troubadour Blacasset laments the death to the secular world of two historically documented courtly ladies, Ugeta and Tefania, who were among the 'joys of Provence', while Pujol celebrates the fact that they will now be dedicating themselves to God. While Carenza is advising Alaisina and Yselda to become brides of Christ, there is nothing mystical about it, Di Luca argues, this being the solution to the wish of Alaisina and Yselda to have a husband but not babies. The image of the two women in the models is turned upside-down: described respectively by Blacasset and Pujol as dead to the world or as saints, in the Alaisina exchange the two women are moved by vanity to choose the cloister over the court, in order to flee the disagreeable consequences of being wives and mothers. Perhaps the name of the counsellor, Carenza, is ironic too, since it means 'deficiency' or 'lack': is she advising the women to do without something?[32] Unfortunately for those who wish to avoid erasing the existence of women troubadours, this interpretation raises serious questions as to the gender of the dialogue's author or authors. Fortunately there are no such doubts concerning the two *trobairitz* with whom this chapter concludes.

Maria de Ventadorn

Daughter of Viscount Raymond II of Turenne and married to the great-grandson of Eble II de Ventadorn 'the singer', Maria de Ventadorn (*c.* 1165 – *c.* 1222) was linked by birth and marriage to families known for their interest in troubadour culture. She was an important patron of troubadours. Bertran de Born, Guiraut de Calanson, the Monk of Montaudon, Pistoleta, Gausbert de Poicibot and Gaucelm Faidit all sang her praises; Bertran referred to her and her two sisters as 'the three of Turenne', lauding their superiority in 'all earthly beauty'. She also participated as arbiter in performances, being called upon to judge three *partimens*, variously involving the troubadours Savaric de Mauléon, Gaucelm Faidit, Uc de la Bacalaria, the Provost of Limoges, Uc de Saint-Circ and Certan, and she herself composed a *partimen* with Gui d'Ussel, her cousin by marriage. His *vida* relates that he shared a castle with his brothers Eble and Peire and his cousin Elias, all troubadours: 'Gui composed good *cansos* and Sir Elias good *tensos*, and Sir Eble the bad *tensos*, and Sir Peire created the tunes to everything the others composed.'[33]

The topic of the *partimen* with Gui,[34] chosen by Maria, is a typical but clever and provocative piece of love casuistry: 'whether, when a lover sincerely asks it of her, a lady is obliged to do equally for him as he ought for her all that pertains to love, according to the code that lovers acknowledge'. Its fame in the thirteenth century may be judged by the existence of two different *razos* about it as well as by the number of manuscripts in which it has been preserved, and it continues to elicit interest in modern readers, being frequently anthologized. It may be the earliest genuine dialogue between a troubadour and a *trobairitz*. Since Maria initiates the debate, Gui chooses which point of view to defend. In accordance with the interest of the male lover he declares that 'the lady is reciprocally obliged to act towards her lover as he towards her, without regard to false pride, for between two lovers there cannot be one greater than the other' (vv. 13–16). Maria's counterarguments astutely exploit the difference between men and women concerning their social situation and power:

> Gui, all that a lover yearns for he must graciously ask for and a lady ought to look favourably on this request, but she is obliged to pay heed to times and seasons. A lover must both beseech and obey as for a friend and, at the same time, for a mistress; whereas a lady ought to honour her lover as a friend but not as a lord and master (vv. 17–24).

There are a great many such debates in the troubadour corpus.[35] The *trobairitz* Guillelma de Rosers and Lanfranc Cigala, an Italian ambassador from Genoa at the court of Provence,[36] debate the following topic: during a storm two knights were on their way to see their ladies when one stopped to help other knights in difficulty, while the other hurried on his way to his beloved. Which of them behaved better?

According to an anonymous *canso* in her praise Guilelma left Provence at some point along with a group of other people and made her way to Genoa, which she seemed to know already. Lanfranc visited the court of Provence in 1241 and their *partimen* may have been composed on this occasion, or else after her transfer to Genoa and before his death in 1257–8.

Isabella

An independently minded and politically ambitious woman, Isabella was probably Italian. Her only known song, a dialogue with the troubadour Elias Cairel, was composed in Greece in 1204–6 in the aftermath of the Fourth Crusade.[37] Though married she was the lover of the Lombard lord Ravano delle Carceri and, after the death of her husband (who remains unknown), they wed in 1212, Pope Innocent III granting them a dispensation despite their adultery on condition that they had not connived at her husband's death. Once the Latins had established their empire in Greece, Ravano served Raimbaut de Vaqueiras's patron the marquis Boniface of Montferrat in Thessalonica and was granted the lordship of Negroponte. Boniface died in 1207 and in the ensuing struggle over which of his sons should become ruler of Thessalonica, Ravano joined other Lombard lords in open revolt against Emperor Henry with the aim of establishing Boniface's son by his first marriage, the new Marquis of Montferrat, William VI, as ruler, thus making Thessalonica independent of Constantinople. Isabella was a keen supporter of this policy, and when William showed little interest in moving to Greece, she used her troubadour to goad him into taking up his inheritance. Elias names various Lombard lords, including Ravano, whom he reports as accusing William of conduct more fitting to a bastard than a legitimate heir, and praises Isabella as the inspirer of knights to perform brave deeds.

He presents one song to 'Lady Isabel' who is 'worth more than all the rest of them', reminding the marquis that 'a dormouse never found its way into the mouth or teeth of a sleeping fox.' Another song, exhorting Emperor Frederick II to go to the Holy Land via Greece, continues to reproach William for his lack of interest in his Greek inheritance, and another is sent, probably from Italy, to a lady 'in Greek lands'. On Ravano's death in 1216 Isabella and her daughter Berta inherited a third of the island of Euboea, and Berta's marriage to Geoffrey of Villehardouin, nephew of the historian of that name and prince of Achaea, proved a shrewd move: their independent principality outlasted that of the kingdom of Thessalonica by more than fifty years.[38]

Isabella initiates her dialogue with Elias by asking why he has directed his amorous attentions elsewhere and no longer celebrates her in his songs.

> 'Sir Elias Cairel, of the love which you and I used to have, I desire you, if you please, to tell me the truth: why have you transferred your attentions to another, for your song is no longer what it once was? And yet I for my part was never for a moment hostile towards you, nor did you ever ask anything of my love that I did not do entirely according to your bidding' (1–8).

Elias replies with amusing frankness that his interest in Isabella was always purely professional, and (somewhat contradictorily) that in any case she has been unreliable in her affections.

> 'My lady Isabella, you used always to uphold reputation, worth, joy, wisdom, and understanding; but if I sang your praises in my verse, I did not do so out of gallantry, but for the reputation and profit I expected from it, as a jongleur

> does from a lady of high renown; but every day *you* have kept being fickle towards *me*' (9–16).

Isabella ripostes that it is unheard-of for a lover of his ardour to abandon a lady for the sake of money, and that she for her part has lost interest in *him*, to which he retorts that he would be mad to stay in her power a moment longer, but in any case he now has a much more physically attractive, loyal and reputable lady than Isabella. Isabella in return accuses him of feigning grief, presumably at her alleged disloyalty, over something 'for which he feels no pain' and advises him to 'go back to living in the abbey'. This sly dig concerning either his impotence or his erotic preferences prompts Elias to switch tack, claiming he has in fact truly suffered for love of her great beauty, but taunting her with a reminder that this will soon fade: 'Lady Isabella, I never dwelt in any monastery, early or late, but you will shortly have occasion to do so, for you will soon lose your looks' (41–4). The song ends with a teasing exchange in which Isabella tempts him to reveal the name of his new lady, hinting at unspecified favours as a way of getting him back: 'If you consented, Sir Elias, I would like you to tell me what manner of woman your beloved is. Tell me now, have no fear, for if she is worth a six [at dice], I will be worth six times more to you' (49–52). Whereupon Elias, as a correct courtly lover fearing the gossipmongers, insists on discretion.

This piece of bantering froth plays openly on the fiction of the troubadour serving his lady for love. Its immediate purpose is entertainment, but it also serves to enhance Isabella's reputation as a woman who can hold court and play at courtly games in a new, fragile geographical and political environment. Elias ends one of his other songs by saying that if the recipient likes it, thanks should go to Lady Isabel, but follows with the words 'No man can sing well without love, yet if I had a merry lady to my liking, I am not in so much despair that I would not love, if I were loved.'[39] This suggests that Elias does not regard Isabella as his beloved, and the idea presented in their dialogue that she ever was is an amusing pretence.

The addressee of the latter song was a highly important figure in Greece at the time: the French poet-musician and crusading commander and diplomat Conon de Béthune, who played the lead in putting down the Lombard revolt. The emperor's life had just been put in grave danger in 1208 when, in the middle of winter, he travelled to Thessalonica to try to obtain the fealty of the Lombards on behalf of Boniface's other son Demetrius. He found his path to Thessalonica blocked. While staying at a monastery 15 kilometres (9 mi.) away, he sent for Conon, who was then about sixty years old and a highly experienced diplomat, to go to talk to the Lombards. Conon succeeded in negotiating Henry's entry into the city and after two months' further negotiations Ravano sent word for a truce, the Lombards yielding all their fiefs and lands to the emperor. At this point Elias tried to mend fences with Conon. The trouvère's song *L'autrier avint en cel autre païs*, which presents an unflattering picture of an older woman upbraiding a knight for falling out of love with her, can be seen as a cleverly veiled political attack on Isabella, who had had no small role in fomenting civil war.[40]

Arnaut Daniel, historiated initial from a *Chansonnier provençal* manuscript, 13th century.

SIX

Arnaut Daniel

In his *Divine Comedy*, Dante (1265–1321) honours Arnaut Daniel above all other vernacular poets before him.[1] He also cites his work in his *De vulgari eloquentia* as a supreme example of illustrious vernacular love poetry, his *L'aur'amara* (IX)[2] as one of the great love poems, his *Sols sui qui sai lo sobrafan qe.m sortz* (XV) as an example of excellent construction and *Si.m fos Amors de joi donar tan larga* (XVII) as a model of the use of the unrhymed stanza.[3] Half a century after Dante's death, Petrarch too, in his *Trionfo d'amore*, proclaimed Arnaut, along with poets writing in Greek, Latin, Italian and Provençal, as a great master of love, still honoured in his own country for his *dir strano e bello*.[4] In modern times he has inspired such poets as Ezra Pound and Jacques Roubaud.[5]

Life and social condition

Little is known about the troubadour's life. He tells us that he attended Philip Augustus of France's coronation in Paris in 1180, and the Monk of Montaudon includes him in his satire on the troubadours, dated to the 1190s.[6] A contemporary and perhaps friend of Bertran de Born, who imitated one of his songs,[7] according to his *razo* he attended the court of Richard the Lionheart in Poitiers. His *vida* states that he was born in the castle of Ribérac (Dordogne), of a noble family, and that after studying (Latin) letters well he took great pleasure in composing songs in the vernacular, abandoning a clerical career for the life of a jongleur.[8] His contemporary Raimon de Durfort referred to him as *Arnaut escolier*, one who is 'ruined by dice and backgammon and goes around like a penitent, poor in clothes and cash' – a description reminiscent of the wandering scholars, the *clerici vagantes* or Goliards brought to life by the translations of Helen Waddell and celebrated in Carl Orff's *Carmina burana*.[9] Raimon treats him as a jongleur ready to carry messages: 'Arnaut scholar, go tonight or tomorrow morning to Lady Enan, and tell her . . .', and the romance of *Flamenca* refers to 'Daniel' as the paragon of jongleuresque art, saying that the hero Guillem de Nevers 'knew more about *cansos* and *lais*, *descortz* and *vers*, *sirventes* and other singing than any jongleur; even Daniel, who knew a great deal, could not be compared with him in the slightest'.[10] Bertran de Born asks an 'Arnautz joglars' to take one of his *sirventes* to Richard the Lionheart, and some critics see this as Arnaut Daniel.[11]

Burlesque and obscenity

All but one of Arnaut's surviving pieces is a love song. The conspicuous exception is his intervention in an obscene and scatalogical dialogue known as 'the Cornilh affair', involving Raimon de Durfort and Truc Malec. A 'lady' has asked her suitor Bernard de Cornilh, as a pledge of his love, to 'trumpet' (*cornar*) her in her backside. On his refusal the three troubadours engage in debate about the rights and wrongs of the affair, deploying a rich vocabulary of body parts, their attributes and actions around them, and an impressive array of rare rhymes and wordplay. What is interesting about the exchange is its links to popular traditions.[12]

Highlighting the fact that the troubadours lived in a pagan-Christian world whose codes, knowledge, practices, belief systems and rituals were very different from the Church's official Christianity, Dominique Pauvert and Christine Escarmant apply the term 'religion carnavalesque' to this universe, which thrived in parallel with, and apparently on the margins of, the one fashioned and recognized by the dominant powers. In medieval carnivalesque festivals, dialogues like this one formed part of the verbal jousts and farce-type plays of which Rabelais later gave many examples. One of these involved wordplay on *còrn* (horn, pipe, anus), which is heavily developed in the troubadour exchange. There still exists a carnivalesque society in the Périgord called the Soufflaculs ('arse-blowers') of Nontron.[13] The French scholars relate that this society originally emerged from Ash Wednesday activities and created the last great carnival of the Périgord under the name of the 'mascarade des Soufflaculs'. This, as in the Occitan exchange, involved the ritual of blowing into the *cul*, which they claim was actually a cosmic, metaphysical act relating to the return of the dead among the living, bringing with them fertility in the form of souls and breaths. The three troubadours, they argue, have used the form of *trobar* to 'faire oeuvre carnavalesque', parodying the ancient carnivalesque rituals and rules.

In the combination of obscene burlesque and dexterous wordplay Arnaut follows a troubadour tradition going back to Guilhem IX and Marcabru, itself emerging from ancient jongleuresque traditions. But such verbal play is by no means confined to popular songs, as it also features in the Latin literature of the medieval schools, and a crossover between the two was already evident in Guilhem's references to the colours of rhetoric Arnaut's knowledge of *letras* overlaps with his skills as a jongleur, both elements feeding into the artistry of the rest of his production, namely his *cansos*.

Trobar car

Arnaut's *vida* and *razo* warn their public that he composed in *caras rimas* such that his songs are difficult to understand and to learn by heart, perhaps picking up on the Monk of Montaudon's satirical dismissal of Arnaut's sophistication: 'he never sang well in all his life except for some nonsensical words that people fail to understand. Since he hunted the hare with the ox and swam against the current, his singing is not worth a rose hip.'[14] Arnaut himself had referred to his own striving after the impossible in these terms.[15] The idea refers to both love and the art of poetry. In all his love songs he searches out rare rhymes and words, and unusual combinations of sound, all interwoven with complex verse forms. Dominique Billy has shown that a quarter of his hundred rhymes listed in Toja's edition are new, that is, unattested in previous generations of troubadours, and at least a tenth of these (*agre*, *ampa*, *ebres*, *éndi*, *int*, *iula*, *òli*, *óma*, *ónc*, *òutas*) are not found in later troubadours either.[16]

Arnaut is the supreme master of the art of interlacing words and rhymes (*entrebescar los motz*), and self-consciously presents himself in this way. Previous troubadours had engaged in intense discussions about literary style, culminating in a debate between Raimbaut d'Aurenga and Guiraut de Borneil about the merits of *trobar clus* and *trobar leu*. Arnaut takes no part in such controversy. His comments on the art of *trobar*, both words and music, focus on the single theme of the unity of art and love. Love inspires him and directs his craft, a craft expressed with terms related to working, polishing, filing, gilding; it commands and teaches him, demanding the highest standard of workmanship, and is both the fruit of art and the guarantor of its perfection:

In this gracious, gay little tune
I fashion words, carpenter and plane,
so that they will be true and certain
when I have passed the file over them;
for Love swiftly smoothes and gilds
my singing, for it proceeds from her
who maintains and upholds reputation (x, 1–7).

High and low among the first leaves
the lands are new with flowers and boughs,
and no bird keeps its beak or throat
mute, but calls and sings,
each according
to its custom.
For the joy I have in them and the season
I sing, but it is Love that delights me
and harmonises words and music. (viii, 1–9).[17]

The song *L'aur'amara* presents an extreme example of his ability to interlace rhymes. Made up of six *coblas unissonans* and a *tornada*, where the rhymes remain constant throughout and where difficult rhymes impose a considerable constraint on the poet, it contains numerous exceptionally short metrical segments, which many editors set out as individual lines but which are here shown as internal rhymes.

L'aur'amara fa.ls bruoils brancutz
clarzir, qe.l douss'espeis'ab fuoills,
e.ls letz becs dels auzels ramencs
ten balps e mutz, pars e non pars;
per q'ieu m'esfortz de far e dir plazers
a mains, per liei que m'a virat bas d'aut,
don tem morir, si.ls afans no m'asoma.

Tant fo clara ma prima lutz
d'eslir lieis don cre.l cors los huoills,
non pretz necs mans dos *aguilencs*;
d'autra s'es dutz rars mos preiars,
pero deportz m'es ad auzir volers,
bos motz ses grei de liei, don tan m'azaut
qu'al sieu servir sui del pe tro q'al coma.[18]

Translated literally, the *canso*'s semantic content is clear, simple and traditional:

> The bitter wind makes the branching thickets grow clear which the gentle one fills out with leaves, and keeps the merry beaks of the birds in the trees, paired and non-paired, stuttering and mute; so I strive to do and say pleasing things to many, for the sake of her who has brought be from low to high, and for whom I fear to die if she does not put an end to my sufferings.
>
> So clear was the first moment my eyes, which the heart believes, lit upon her, that I prize secret messages not two rose hips; rarely have my prayers been inspired by another, but it is a pleasure for me to hear wishes, lovely words without reproach, from the one in whom I delight so much that I am at her service from head to foot.

The nature opening motivates a request for love in the form of song, and is followed by praise of the lady's beauty and the poet's profession of exclusive devotion to her service. But the elaboration of these topoi is exceptional in its striving for formal and stylistic density. Mimicking the stuttering of the birds (*balps*), the stanza proceeds in a series of fitful oppositions: the winter wind/spring's leafy branches, lightening and thickening (*clarzir*/

espeis'), bitter and gentle (*amara/douss'*), birds merry or mute (*letz/mutz*), paired and non-paired (*pars/non pars*), the changes in the speaker's status from low to high (*bas/aut*), the switch from being 'high' (*aut*) to the fear of death (*tem morir*), and from suffering (*afans*) to the lady ending it (*asoma*). All this spikiness is reinforced by monosyllables, outnumbering polysyllables in this stanza by three to one, and by tight or harsh sounds (*letz, becs, bas d'aut, bruoils brancutz*), full of echoes, *letz becs dels auzels ramencs*, for instance. Only two full words have the more free-flowing feminine ending (*amara, asoma*), strikingly occurring at the very beginning and end of the stanza. The brief smooth sound flow of *l'aur'amara* is immediately undercut by the sense of *amara*, 'bitter' and the harsh consonants that follow, while the end word, *asoma*, brings a sense of pause, ending and relief. But it also contains an echo of *som*, which can mean both 'dream' and 'summit', and *soma*, 'sum' or 'sum total', so the listener might think also of the suitor hoping his lady will induce in him a dream-like state, or else bring him to the summit (of joy) beyond the *aut* of the penultimate line. The oppositions fuse, perhaps.

The blend of 'smooth-combed' and 'shaggy' or rough words (*vocabula pexa atque yrsuta*) was something that Dante particularly praised in the troubadours. Peire d'Alvernhe was the first to combine these in love songs, with the rougher sounds of *trobar brau*, found mainly in moralizing poetry, giving 'a slight abrasiveness and richening of texture to harmoniously smooth sounds' and suggesting 'not blame and discord but intellectual and moral effort'.[19] Arnaut's piece explicitly highlights effort – *per q'ieu m'esfortz de far e dir plazers* – but the effect in his opening stanza takes this idea further to create a mood of inner struggle.

The 'sestina'

The combination of formal complexity and rare rhymes attains new heights in Arnaut's song *Lo ferm voler qu'el cor m'intra* (XVIII), which later became known as the first 'sestina' and which inspired many poets, Occitan, Italian and others, to imitate it.[20] To help readers unfamiliar with medieval Occitan the better to appreciate its shape and sound patterns it is presented here in its edited Occitan form, followed by an English translation that attempts, however imperfectly, to follow the rhyme scheme and rhythm of the original, insofar as flexible English blank verse is susceptible to this.

I

Lo ferm voler qu'el cor m'intra
no.m pot ges becs escoissendre ni ongla
de lauzengier qui pert per mal dir s'arma:
e pus non l'aus batr'ab ram ni ab verja,
sivals a frau, lai on non aurai oncle,
jauzirai joi, en vergier o dins cambra.

II

Quan mi sove de la cambra
on a mon dan sai que nulhs om non intra
– ans me son tug plus que fraire ni oncle –
non ai membre no·m fremisca, neis l'ongla,
aissi cum fai l'enfas devant la verja:
tal paor ai no·l sia prop de l'arma.

III

Del cors li fos, non de l'arma,
e cossentis m'a celat dins sa cambra,
que plus mi nafra·l cor que colp de verja
qu'ar lo sieus sers lai on ilh es non intra;
de lieis serai aisi cum carns et ongla,
e non creirei castic d'amic ni d'oncle.

IV Anc la seror de mon oncle
non amei plus ni tan, per aqest'arma,
21 qu'aitan vezis cum es lo detz de l'ongla,
s'a lieis plagues, volgr'esser de sa cambra;
de me pot far l'amors q'ins el cor m'intra
24 miels a son vol c'om fortz de frevol verja.

V Pus flori la seca verja
ni de n'Adam foron nebot ni oncle,
27 tant fin'amors cum selha qu'el cor m'intra
non cug fos anc en cors no neis en arma;
on qu'eu estei, fors en plan o dins cambra,
30 mos cors no·s part de lieis tant cum ten l'ongla.

VI Aissi s'empren s s'enongla
mos cors en lieis cum l'escors'en la verja,
33 qu'ilh m'es de joi tors e palais e cambra;
e non am tan paren, fraire ni oncle,
qu'en Paradis n'aura doble joi m'arma,
36 si ja nuilhs hom per ben amar lai intra.

VII Arnautz tramet son cantar d'ongl'e d'oncle,
a grat de lieis qui de sa verj'a l'arma,
39 son desirat, qu'apres, en cambra intra

I The firm desire which in my heart enters
no beak can ever tear apart, nor nail
3 of slanderer, whose smears lose him his soul;
since I dare not strike him with branch or rod,
save secretly, there where there is no uncle
6 I'll have my joy in orchard or in chamber.

II When I recall the chamber
where to my harm I know that no man enters
9 – for all oppose me more than brother or uncle –
no part of me's not trembling, even nail,
just as the child trembles before the rod:
12 so much I fear not being close in soul.

III Would I were close in body, not soul,
and secretly she let me in her chamber!
15 It wounds my heart more than a blow of rod
that now where she is her servant does not enter:
I shall be hers just as with flesh and nail,
18 and heed no remonstrance from friend or uncle.

IV Never the sister of my uncle
loved I more or so much, by this my soul,
21 For close as is the finger to the nail,
if it pleased her, would I be to her chamber:
more can the love which enters in my heart
24 do as it wills than strong man with frail rod.

V Since there flowered the dry rod
and from Sir Adam sprang nephew or uncle,
27 such fine love which in my heart enters
was I think never found in body or yet soul;
where'er I am, outside or within chamber,
30 my heart/body parts not from her the length
of a nail.

VI Thus my heart/body takes hold like a nail
and grafts itself in her like bark in rod;
33 of joy she is my tower, palace, chamber,
and more I love not parent, brother, uncle;

for double joy in Paradise will fill my soul,
36 if any man for loving well there enters.

VII Arnaut transmits his song of nail and uncle,
to please the one possessing his rod's soul,
39 the song desired which, learned, in chamber enters.[21]

The degree of formal complexity here is unprecedented. The challenge Arnaut set himself was to use the same set of whole, rare rhyme-words throughout, but to rearrange the order in which they appear in each successive stanza in an elegant and satisfying way. There are six lines in each stanza and each line has a different rhyme-word. If he had simply wished for each stanza to have the six rhyme-words in a different order there could be as many as 720 stanzas. In the context of bellringing, a full peal on six bells would last for 720 rounds; one possible such sequence is known as the Full Bob Minor. Arnaut had in mind a more elegant procedure in which the *rearrangement* of the order of rhyme-words between successive stanzas should be the same each time, and each rhyme-word should appear once in each stanzaic position. This implies that the number of stanzas in the rhyme scheme must be the same as the number of lines per stanza. In six stanzas there are still 120 (5×4×3×2×1) possible permutations to choose from. A less interesting and ambitious choice than the one adopted would be *abcdef* → *bcdefa*, where each rhyme word sinks by one line from each stanza to the next until it reaches the bottom and then jumps to the first line. Arnaut preferred something producing a less obvious sequence, while still retaining the discipline of a single fixed permutation.

His choice of order could be envisaged in terms of card games – presumably not in his experience, since card games only seem to have reached Europe in the late fourteenth century. When we want to disrupt patterns and produce some appearance of randomness we shuffle the cards. A commonly used basic shuffle is the riffle shuffle, where the pack is divided into equal halves that are then combined by alternating cards from the two parts. For a six-card pack *abcdef* this permutation would be either *adbecf* or *daebfc*, depending on which part begins the alternations. Arnaut uses what could be regarded as a simple modification of a riffle shuffle, with the second part being flipped upside down: the six rhyme-words are divided into two sets of three, *abc* and *def*; the second set is reversed to *fed*, and the two resulting sets are shuffled together as *faebdc*, so *a,b,c* go into positions 2,4,6 (see diagram below). The permutation has replaced *a* by *f*, *b* by *a*, *c* by *e*, and so on, as shown in the right-hand diagram, which shows that if one were to apply this permutation six times one would arrive back at the original order.[22]

A different way of explaining this pattern, closer to Arnaut's putative experience, is to envisage it as a dance. The dancers join hands in a straight line and then stand still. The dancer at the back peels off, starting and leading a new line by picking up dancers alternately from the front and the back of the old line, until the process is complete and there is a single new line. Six

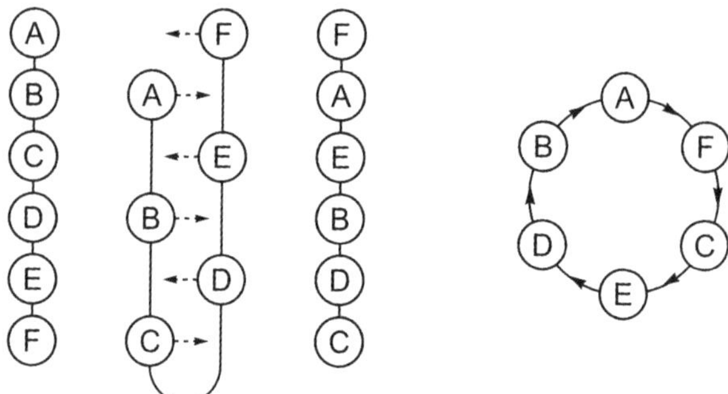

The permutations of rhyme-words from each stanza to the next. The sequence is first folded back on itself and then the two halves are merged together. The new sequence can be seen as replacing each rhyme-word by the next in the cycle illustrated on the right.

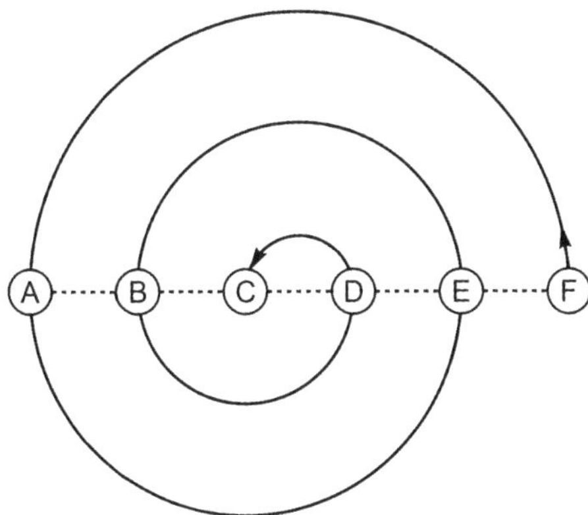

A hypothetical dance sequence.

repetitions of this would bring the dancers back to their original order.[23]

Arnaut has chosen the particular rhyme-words for various reasons. First, they are all bisyllables with a feminine ending with the stress on the first syllable: an unusual choice, which here generates a pause at the end of each line, inducing the listener to linger over the key word. Second, all are rare. And third, they express and steer a line of thought. The troubadours called this the song's *razo*.

The words *intra* and *cambra* encapsulate the poet's desire for union with the object of his desire, and evoke the common medieval trope of the earthly paradise or *locus amoenus*. *Oncle* is difficult to integrate as the *razo* unfolds. First of all it serves to represent the beloved's kin impeding his access to her. In stanzas III, IV and VI it refers to his own kin, and in V it becomes part of the history of all mankind. Both IV and VI introduce an element of self-conscious humour, Arnaut somewhat tortuously representing his mother as his uncle's sister and Adam's seed as a succession of nephews and uncles. *Verga* introduces the idea of pain or punishment (stanzas I–IV), but also takes on erotic connotations, one of its meanings being 'penis' (V–VII). *Ongla* echoes *oncle* in both sound and sense, representing in turn the sharp tongues of the hostile slanderers and gossips (*lauzengiers*) who stand in the way of love's consummation, and parts of the lover's own body, whether fearful (II) or in imagined union with his beloved (III, IV, VI). *Arma* introduces a spiritual aspect to the love theme, first appearing as the 'sinful' (in lovers' terms) *lauzengiers* losing their soul (I). In stanzas II–III it expresses the lover's fear that his love will remain purely spiritual, and in IV it is integrated into the playful lines where Arnaut hints at finding his rhyme scheme something of a challenge. By stanzas V–VI the carnal and spiritual sides of his love unite in *fin'amors*: 'there never was such love in body or even soul', and his *cors*, meaning both heart and body, is always entirely with her. Finally he presents the status of his eternal soul as equivocal, for his anticipation of double joy in the next life is conditional: does loving well grant entry? Despite Dante's unqualified admiration for Arnaut as a poet, he placed him in Purgatory, not Paradise, among the lustful.

The *tornada* offers different senses in different manuscripts. In the modern edition followed here, the word *son* is the song itself, which on its conclusion enters the beloved's chamber.[24] However, *desirat* has often been taken to be a *senhal* or pseudonym, so the version meaning 'to his Desired One' (the form being masculine) would refer either to the lady herself or to the troubadour Bertran de Born.[25]

Music and performance

From his analysis of Arnaut's surviving music Francesco Carapezza concludes that his activity as a jongleur, attested by his contemporaries and the later tradition, indicates experience in the performative side of *trobar*. Numerous musical references in his pieces, some quite unusual, reinforce this idea and make

Lo ferm voler, musical notation from a *Chansonnier provençal* manuscript, early 14th century.

one envisage him as a composer who knew the cultivated musical tradition of his time, and the representation of Arnaut as a practised jongleur is likely to be based on genuine information. Further support for this, he suggests, is the fact that he signs his name within one of his songs. At the same time, his pictorial portrait in the Venetian songbooks AIK (known as manuscripts) show him dressed as a schoolmaster, the illuminator of manuscript A writing in the margin '.I. maistro cun capa crespa' (a master with a ruffled robe). This contrasts with the tradition of an 'Arnaut jongleur' and instead seems conditioned by his status as *litteratus*. His 'sestina' is one of two pieces whose melody is transmitted in manuscript G. Here Carapezza sees Arnaut's musical devices as 'sober but effective', counterbalancing the harmonic artifices and innovative metaphors of his *trobar car*.[26]

SEVEN

Bertran de Born

Bertran's songs are mainly political *sirventes*. They centre on his lived experience as a minor nobleman of the Aquitaine aristocracy, and his life and compositions are intimately intertwined. Of immense vitality, his poems speak across the centuries, illuminating their time and place. Yet we need some knowledge of their time and place to understand more than their surface. He was closely involved in the political and family affairs of the Plantagenets, and his works are an essential historical source for our understanding of events taking place in late twelfth-century Aquitaine. Much more is known about this troubadour than many others, but ironically, the more we know, the more we are aware of not knowing. The two modern editions consulted for this chapter are both indispensable and non-definitive.[1]

Hautefort

Bertran's family held the fortress (*castrum*) of Hautefort in the Dordogne. Unlike the grand seventeenth-century reconstruction that stands today, the castle probably consisted of a keep and great hall surrounded by an enclosure (*verteilh*) containing dwellings for the knights in charge of local defence, cabins for domestics, stables and barns. It had a chapel dedicated to the Virgin, and a chaplaincy.[2]

Bertran de Born, historiated initial from a *Chansonnier provençal* manuscript, 13th century.

When Bertran was born in around 1140, his family did not own it. They held it as lords or castellans from the family of the Lastours *principes*, who possessed it as part of their ancestral estates. Just before 1180, our troubadour became head of the Born lineage and sole head of Hautefort. For many years the *vidas* and *razos* led to the mistaken belief that Bertran shared Hautefort with his brother Constantin under a system of indivision, common elsewhere in the Midi, whereby all male heirs shared equally in the family estates. The Borns were closely related to the more powerful Lastours through intermarriage, and when Bertran became master of Hautefort, Constantin was probably living not there but at Lastours, with his wife Agnes of Lastours and their family. The two brothers (a third, Itier, disappears from records after 1169) would find themselves in dispute, not because they were sharing the castle, which they were not, but because of dissensions among the Lastours themselves over inheritance issues. In order to preserve the primacy of their small son over the children of their cousin Seguin, who was married to Bertran's daughter Aimeline, Agnes and her brother Gouffier pressed Constantin to assert not a hypothetical indivision but the ancient rights that the Lastours had always had over the fortress.[3]

When he took over the command of Hautefort, Bertran was married with at least three children and approaching the age of forty. The region was beset by war: war between local barons, war between Aragon and Toulouse, mercenary bands living by pillage and hire, internecine war among the Plantagenets, and rebellions against Richard the Lionheart's rule of Aquitaine. As Gérard Gouiran observes,

> the history of this duchy is a long series of rebellions subdued with varying degrees of difficulty. Conflicts between local lords overlap with the chronic opposition between Aquitainian vassals and their Angevin suzerains, playing a not negligible role in the rivalry which sets Capetians against Plantagenets during what has been called the first Hundred Years' War.[4]

During these upheavals Bertran, a supporter of the local rebels, lost his castle twice: once in 1182, when Richard made him hand it over to Constantin, and again in 1183 after a seven-day siege by Richard in person with the help of his ally King Alfonso II of Aragon. A judgement of Henry II not only returned it to the troubadour but in 1184 made him a direct vassal of the king of France, and the lordship of Hautefort passed for the first time into the hands of a Born.

Bertran and the Plantagenets: schism and revolt

Eleanor of Aquitaine, granddaughter of the first troubadour, had inherited her duchy in 1137 from William X at the age of seventeen. She was immediately married to Louis VII, king of France. Their marriage ended in divorce in 1152, when Henry

Plantagenet, king of England two years later, snapped up this valuable heiress. On 6 January 1169 he theoretically divested himself of his continental domains, and officially made his sons vassals of the king of France. The young Henry was designated heir to Normandy, Anjou and Maine; Richard, Eleanor's favourite, was officially recognized as her heir in Aquitaine; Brittany was assigned to Geoffrey, who paid homage to his eldest brother for it, while the much younger John remained without inheritance. A year later, in June 1170, and again in 1172, Henry II had the young Henry crowned king as heir to his father's patrimony,[5] but the Young King remained without lands and depended on a paternal allowance. During 1171–2 Eleanor presented Richard as her heir throughout her duchy and enthroned him during grand ceremonies. Then, in February 1173, Henry II made it clear that he had not after all given up sovereignty over his continental domains, and his sons had their titles only as his delegates. The three elder brothers, no doubt incited by Eleanor, revolted. Eleanor was captured in November 1173, imprisoned at Chinon, then held under house arrest in Salisbury castle for some fifteen years, while at Christmas in 1174 Henry pardoned his sons for their rebellion. None of all this yet posed a direct threat to Hautefort, but it would do so later, when the Young King, envious of Richard's resources and independence, would side with the rebel barons of Aquitaine.[6]

When Richard took over as ruler in 1175, he was determined to import into his duchy foreign vassalic practices that curtailed the local barons' traditional independence. He soon faced uprisings in Gascony and then, in the spring of 1176, the Angoumois and Limousin. Viscount Ademar V of Limoges took a prominent role in this and all subsequent uprisings. Bertran does not seem to have participated in the 1176 coalition, but must have been aware of events taking place on his doorstep; in early 1177 an army of Richard's mercenaries devastated the region of Yssaudon, less than 20 kilometres (12 mi.) away from Hautefort. Then, with their camp followers of concubines and prostitutes, they besieged and occupied the castle of Malemort, from where they terrorized the inhabitants of the lower Limousin. A few weeks later the religious authorities of the region called on the population to take up arms, and they massacred 2,000 brigands, male and female. A few months later Henry II came south to settle matters and reduced Ademar's remaining shreds of autonomy, forcing him to hand the castle of Limoges to Richard's officers.[7]

After a relative lull in 1178–80, revolt broke out again. When Vulgrin of Angoulême died in 1181 leaving a young daughter as sole direct heir, Richard forcefully asserted his right to act as her ward, and drove Vulgrin's brothers, who expected to inherit the city according to local custom, out of town. The rebels 'formed a league with a great oath sworn on a missal in an ancient church of Saint Martial',[8] and in 1182 Bertran the troubadour entered the scene with a great rallying-cry.

Since Ventadorn, and Comborn with Segur,
and Turenne, and Montfort with Gourdon
have joined with Périgueux and sworn alliance,
and burghers all around lock themselves in,
it pleases me to sing and undertake
a *sirventes* to give them reassurance:
I would not want Toledo to be mine
if I could not live there in security.

Ah, Puy-Guilhem and Clérans and Grignols
and Saint-Astier, you act with highest honour,
and so do I, if this were acknowledged,
and Angoulême outstandingly – more so
than Sir Carter who is abandoning the cart!
He has no money and takes none without fear;

so I prize more a scrap of land with honour
than holding a great empire with dishonour.

If the powerful viscount, head of the Gascons,
on whom depend Béarn and the Gabardan,
and Sir Vezian and Sir Bernard wish it,
with the lord of Dax and the ruler of Marsan,
over here the count will have plenty to do;
and in the same way, just as he is valiant,
with the great army he is gathering and amassing,
let him ride here and come to our side![9]

Bertran salutes the instigators of the resistance, then calls on men elsewhere in Richard's domains to join in, taunting the impecunious Young King ('Sir Carter'), who depends on his father's allowance and is too cowardly to take what is due to him by force,[10] and goading him by mentioning the castle of Clairvaux, recently built by Richard on land strategically situated between the Young King's Maine, Richard's Poitou and Geoffrey's Brittany.

The Young King's rivalry with his younger brother led him to hesitate between supporting Richard or the rebels. Some chroniclers report that he fled to his brother-in-law the king of France; at any rate he seems to have gone off tourneying with him. Bertran intensifies his jibes: he has heard the extraordinary news that the Young King has given up what he was demanding of Richard because his father told him to! Accusing him of cowardice in 'living entirely on handouts that are counted and measured out',[11] he jeers that sleeping is not how the young man will be king of the English, or conquer Ireland, or hold Anjou, or be duke of Normandy. With bitter sarcasm he encourages Richard to continue doing exactly what he is doing.

I want to give advice to the tune of 'Lady Alamanda',
to Sir Richard over there, even if he's not asking me
for it:
he should never treat his men favourably on his brother's
account.
And neither does he! Instead he sets siege, erodes their
possessions,
steals their castles and demolishes and burns
on all sides.
Let the king go tourneying with the men of Garlanda,
and the other one, his brother-in-law.[12]

In the event Henry II persuaded the Young King to return, and he attended the elder king's Christmas court of Caen in 1182. Bertran also attended, perhaps summoned to explain himself as a result of these two *sirventes*.[13] He was made to hand Hautefort over to his brother Constantin, one of Richard's supporters. Further quarrels sparked a general conflagration. This time it involved powers outside Aquitaine, bringing armies, including mercenaries, from France, Burgundy, Toulouse, Aragon and Catalonia, which devastated the Limousin. The Young King rejoined the rebels, and commissioned Bertran to rouse people in their support. Then on 11 June 1183 the Young King suddenly died. Bertran composed a *planh* for his death. The war was over, and Richard, in the company of Alfonso of Aragon, an old ally of the Plantagenets and constant enemy of the count of Toulouse, set off to ravage the lands of the count of Périgord, when Bertran lost Hautefort for the second time.[14]

We do not know how he persuaded the king not only to return it to him but to detach it from dependency on the Lastours. Was Henry moved by the troubadour's lament for his eldest son?[15] Was it the result of Bertran's wits, of which he boasts?[16] Whatever the case, the troubadour made his peace with Richard. From then on, he enthusiastically supported his wars against his brother-in-law Philip of France.

The *sirventes* and war poetry

The term *sirventes* seems fluid at Bertran's time, for he calls one war song a *canso* and refers to another as both *canso* and *sirventes*.[17] The genre dealt with a variety of political and moralizing topics involving exhortation, and praise or blame, following in the tradition of Marcabrunian vituperation. It included insult poetry, whether playfully directed at a luckless jongleur or attacking one's enemies. One such target was the king of Aragon, Alfonso II,[18] who took part in the siege of Hautefort in 1183. The troubadour casts aspersions on his birth, accuses him of coming for purely mercenary reasons, robbing people of their rightful lands, mistreating jongleurs and yawning at the prospect of battle, and tells him to go off and seek his fortune in the Holy Land – though he is such a cowardly weakling he is bound to be seasick on the way! Bertran may have met Alfonso earlier in friendlier circumstances, which could explain the report in one of this troubadour's *vidas* that 'the king of Aragon gave Guiraut de Borneil's *cansos* as wives to his *sirventes*.' Because Bertran was the first troubadour to compose *sirventes* modelled on the tune and verse form of *cansos*, Carapezza argues that the *vida* was referring to the practice of setting *sirventes* to *cansos* melodies. Bertran is explicit about this when he sets *D'un sirventes no.m cal far loignor ganda* 'to the tune of Lady Alamanda' by Guiraut de Borneil.[19]

Dante celebrated Bertran as the poet of arms *par excellence*. In his *De vulgari eloquentia* it suited his purposes to present him as a vernacular example of one of the three great poetic themes of Classical antiquity: *salus* (safety), *venus* (love) and *virtus* (righteousness). In his *Divine Comedy*, however, he consigned him to the flames of hell, among the sowers of discord (*scandalo*) and schism. His shadow appears to Dante as a headless trunk, condemned eternally to carry by his hair his severed head, which swings in his hand like a lantern. His punishment mirrors his sin of making father and son 'rebels to each other': 'Because I parted persons thus united, I carry my brain, alas! separated from its source which is in this trunk.' Stefano Asperti shows that Dante was drawing here on texts of a later time, wrongly attributed to this troubadour, which makes a difference to the tone of Bertran's war poetry, for these texts of doubtful authenticity are more violent, brutal or gruesome than those of assured authorship.[20] So was Dante right to damn our troubadour as a 'sower of schism and discord'?

There can hardly be any doubt that Bertran aimed to get the Young King to join the southern rebels against Richard and the Old King. In fairness, one might argue that he was justified in defending his own *salus*. But it is not only in this context that he glorifies war. 'I always want the great barons to be angry with each other,' he proclaims in a song commissioned by Count Raymond v of Toulouse during conflict with Alfonso of Aragon.[21] During conflicts between Richard the Lionheart and Philip of France he blames Philip for wanting peace: 'War, waged without fire and blood by a king or a powerful lord who is being insulted and thwarted, is in no way a pretty word! Let him rest and get fat later. A young man who does not feed on war easily gets flabby and base.' Richard is praiseworthy because, unlike Philip, he is always passionately in favour of war.[22] When both are at peace, Bertran goads them to resume fighting:

Since the barons are irritated and upset
over this peace that the two kings have made,
I shall make a song so when they learn of it
each one will be impatient to wage war.
It displeases me for a king to stay in peace,

Richard the Lionheart and Philip of France, miniature from William of Tyre, *La conquête de la Terre sainte*, 13th century.

> disinherited and denied his rights,
> without conquering what he's justly claimed . . .
> For a king to seek negotiation, once he's armed
> and in the field, is considered to be weakness.
> From what I hear, Burgundians and French
> have certainly exchanged honour for greed,
> and it would be better, by the faith I owe you,
> for king Philip to give the signal to attack
> than parley in his armour by the river.[23]

And after Richard's coronation on 3 September 1189 he drives the new king to make more conquests instead of living the soft life, where he 'brandishes goblets and drinking-cups, and pots of silver and kettles, and haunts rivers and forests – and here he used to take and give! He should not swerve from suffering: mêlées and tumult, wars and disorder will be to his advantage.'[24]

So why does Bertran want to disrupt the peace? War, he affirms, stimulates courts, courting and gift-giving. In peacetime, 'Handsome people and fine armour can be plentifully seen and found . . . and plenty with smooth-combed hair, polished teeth and moustaches on their faces, but there is no-one who knows how to love, hold a court, woo ladies or give generously.'[25] Generous spending is certainly part of the attraction. In peacetime the members of the upper nobility (*rics*) turn inward to improving the comforts of their estates, 'uprooting bushes, they

Bertran in hell, drawing by Gustave Doré, 1861.

love orchards and gardens so much'; living a life of ease and privacy, 'they seem to be protecting themselves from the Assassins, for you will never enter without a brawl into wherever any of them is to be found.'[26] There is more to his promotion of war than self-defence. 'Don't think I'm fomenting discord with my accusations,' he declares, 'if I want the *rics* to hate each other, as vavassors and castellans can have more joy of them. A great man is more affable, open-handed and friendly in times of war than in peacetime.'[27]

He revels in the Young King's entourage with its free spending and intimacy with the great, the glamour of 'courts and exploits and the joy of love'. Henry is the ideal nobleman: 'generous and well-spoken, a fine horseman, handsome, kindly in bestowing great honours', the leader of courtly *joven* and the generous source of 'hauberks and swords, fine buckrams, helmets and pennons, pourpoints and cloths and joy and love'. With his death Bertran laments the disappearance of the courtly life Henry epitomized: 'a gracious welcome, gift-giving with no hidden motive, a courteous reply and word of welcome, a spacious inn, paid for and well-kept, gifts and arms and no wrong-doing, dining to the sound of the viol and song, and many a companion, spirited and powerful from society's elite'.[28]

Asperti argues that Dante, in his *Divine Comedy*, criticizes through Bertran and other poetry in his 'style' the values he sees embodied in a certain knightly culture.[29] The question then arises: what is Bertran's relationship to contemporary concepts of knighthood and chivalry?

Knighthood and chivalry

As an elite professional horseback warrior, the knight was a universal phenomenon in Europe by the end of the eleventh century. He required access to the resources to equip himself with a horse and specialized armour, but he did not need to be highborn or wealthy, since a leader seeking promising recruits might provide this equipment. As time went on, however, knights began to be marked off as an exclusive caste, entry into which was marked by noble birth and solemn rituals. These might involve religious elements such as the presence of an altar, as well as such secular gestures as the girding on of the sword with the belt of knighthood. By the thirteenth century accession to knighthood came to be an extremely expensive affair, and young noblemen might serve a period of apprenticeship as squires before becoming knights – some never choosing to make the transition. For most of the twelfth century, however, squires were simply ordinary servants performing rather menial jobs, looking after horses and armour, running errands, performing domestic chores and foraging and ravaging in warfare. It was only in the thirteenth century that literature shows a squire being knighted.

Bertran never specifies his own social condition, though he places himself among vavassors or *pros paubres*, poor but worthy men, out of range of a high-born *domna* who can choose one of the most noble castellans or rich barons for her suitor.[30] While he celebrates Richard's wars, he claims to be too poor to join in: 'I would have received blows on my shield and made my white standard crimson,' he declares, but 'I possess neither Lusignan nor Rancon to enable me to go waging war without wealth.'[31] In his poems of secure attribution the term *cavaller* applies either to professional horseback warriors who are retained by the *rics*, or to a lady's suitor.[32] In the latter case, the category must be a broad one, including anyone who fights on horseback, from a simple retainer to a high nobleman. There is little to suggest that knighthood for Bertran implies a special caste with its own rituals or chivalric ethos.

The Third Crusade

In 1187 Bertran, along with the trouvère Conon de Béthune,[33] was caught up in the wave of impassioned responses in the West to the fall of Jerusalem. The pope called for a new crusade, while in the Holy Land Conrad of Montferrat courageously defended Tyre against Saladin, sending desperate pleas for help to the West. Richard immediately took the cross. Bertran exhorted men to follow God's summons, and praised Richard's leadership:

> Our Lord Himself issues the summons
> to all the bold and valiant and prized,
> for war nor mêlée never caused Him grief,
> yet He holds Himself much grieved by this one.
> The true cross and the king are captive,
> and the sepulchre is bereft of aid,
> where all of us believe with firm true faith
> the holy fire descends: people can see it,
> so there is no difficulty in believing.
>
> The one who is count and duke and will be king
> has stepped forward, so his merit doubles,
> for he loves merit more than all of the two faiths,
> the Christians and the non-baptised.[34]

Other leaders showed less sense of urgency. The kings of England and France continued to wage war on each other and hence delayed the arrival of help to Conrad in Tyre, and Richard too was in no hurry to depart. The delays caused a storm of protest. At the end of the spring of 1188 Bertran allots praise and blame: 'Now it will be clear who has the greatest merit of all the early risers: Lord Conrad's is the purest and the truest, defending

Effigy of Richard the Lionheart, Royal Abbey of Fontevraud.

himself overseas in Tyre against Lord Saladin and his vile troops. God will help him, for help is slow in coming! He alone will have the prize, since he alone suffers the hardship.'[35] Despite his exhortations, Bertran himself did not join the Third Crusade. He offers what seems like a rather lame excuse: 'Lord Conrad, to Jesus I commend you, for I would be there at your side, I assure you, but I held back when I saw the greatest men, the kings and princes, were taking up the cross. Then I saw my lovely blond lady, who makes my heart grow weak – but I would be with you if I knew as much about it as they do.'[36] Jean-Pierre Thuillat is inclined to take this at face value, and suggests that the troubadour's 'lovely blond lady' is his second wife whom he had recently married. This is not impossible, but the courtly trope of the beloved holding a man back from crusading, often the subject of blame by both ecclesiastical preachers and troubadours, looks somewhat casual here, and in the last line Bertran is hinting at much left unsaid.[37]

Love

Although his songs are predominantly political, about one-fifth are love poems, and most of his compositions contain love elements. As Gouiran observes, this is less a sign of personal temperament than of the fact that the role of love was so important in medieval Occitan life that it could not be confined to personal pieces: whether real or imagined, it stamped its mark on all other activities. The main thing for Bertran in his love poetry, along with a competitive element – his lady has to be the best – is physical beauty, which he sometimes expresses in somewhat startling or abrupt terms.[38] In a request for love, a standard element of the *canso*, he takes a more than usually direct approach: 'Lady whose heart is stingy with promises and gifts, since you do not wish to lie with me, give me a kiss!' His praise of Matilda of Saxony, duchess and daughter of Henry II, is surprising:

> Her joyful, youthful, gracious, loving body does not rely for its beauty on deceit or illusion. It becomes more lovely still if you unlace her, and the more you were to remove her clothes, the more you would desire her, for her throat turns night into day – and if you could see further down, the whole world would be more beautiful.[39]

This was one of two pieces composed in Normandy during winter 1182–3, when Bertran had just been forced to hand Hautefort over to Constantin. It seems he was more or less constrained to be there, perhaps because Richard did not want to leave him behind in the south to stir up trouble, or because Henry II had summoned him to explain himself over his songs of revolt.[40] Thuillat suggests that Richard may have used the troubadour to keep his sister entertained. Whatever the case, Bertran enjoyed rubbing shoulders with the great, boasting that his lord (Richard or Henry?) had seated him next to the duchess 'on an imperial cushion'.[41] Apart from Matilda's company, however, he failed to enjoy her court at Argentan:

> A court will never be perfect where people don't joke or laugh. A court without gifts is nothing but a park of barons. The disagreeable, coarse behaviour (*l'enois e la vilania*) at Argentan would have been the death of me, but that the noble, lovable person and the sweet kind face and the good company and conversation of the Saxon lady protected me.[42]

Editors have taken the word *enois* to mean 'boredom', but its coupling with *vilania* suggests some unpleasantness towards Bertran during his stay.

Sometimes the love theme is simply an afterthought, connecting him to the courtly community.[43] But the blend of the political and amorous can be more complex. The nature opening of *Al nou doutz termini blanc*, with hints of *trobar clus* through rare words and a difficult rhyme-scheme, leads to the expectation of a love song, which develops into the invocation of a 'gracious promise': a promise of love?

> In the new, sweet, white season
> I see the most exquisite signs of spring
> filling the new time with delight,
> when the days are more gracious,
> more pleasurable and more prized,
> and people should be merrier,
> and when I find more savour in joy.
>
> So, at a standstill, I am unhappy
> not to be quickly leaving the feast-day behind.

A single day seems like thirty to me
because of a gracious promise
which brings me trouble and alarm;
I don't wish Douai to be mine
without the hope of having Cambrai.

Douai and Cambrai seem at first to be metaphors for his lady's favours, but it soon becomes apparent that they are meant literally, as cities under contention during the wars of Richard and Philip. The language becomes anything but courtly: 'A stye and tumour in the eye to anyone who urges him [Philip] to act like this! Miserable cowardice will not avail him as much as noble spending, nor will rest and leisure as much as war, effort and suffering!'[44]

In *Quan la novella flors par el vergan* he again plays with some of the typical conventions of the courtly *canso*, such as the nature opening and the expression of desire:

When the fresh flower appears on the branch,
where the twigs are scarlet, green and white,
with the sweetness I feel at the turn of the year,
I sing just as the other birds do,
for I take myself as a bird in many ways,
since I dare to desire all the best there is in the world.
I dare to desire it and to have a yearning heart,
but I dare not tell her/him my heart; instead I hide it from
her/him.[45]

The rhyme scheme, key rhyme sounds and rhyme words (*volon*, *rescon*, *mon*, *desiron*, *respon*), and the identification of the poet with a bird echo Bernart de Ventadorn's *Can vei la lauzeta mover*.[46] Bertran's ploddingly explicit comparison, however – 'I take myself as a bird in many ways' – contrasts with the delicacy of Bernart's metaphor, generating the comical rationale of being a bird because one dares to desire 'the best' – a play in turn on the ideal of 'the best' (*lo mieills*) found in early troubadours such as Guilhem IX, and interpretable in earthy as well as idealistic ways. The introduction ends with a further play on *canso* commonplaces, namely the lover's timidity, but the indeterminate gender of the one from whom the poet conceals his desire introduces an ambiguity that is promptly exploded in what follows. 'I am not a lover,' he announces flatly, 'nor do I pretend [both 'aspire' and 'feign'] to speak or appeal to any lady, nor do I woo' (9–11). 'Since a man without a *domna* cannot compose a love song,' he continues, 'I shall make a fresh new *sirventes*' (17–18), castigating Geoffrey of Brittany for abandoning the Limousin barons' revolt against Richard. His 'desire' thus proves to be political and military, and at the point where he sends his *sirventes* off to Catalonia, it is his friend the troubadour Guilhem de Berguedà, not a woman, who has been the source of *fin joi*, true or courtly joy (45–6).

Bertran's poetic impact

None of Bertran's songs can be securely dated to before 1182, during the uprising in the Limousin when he was about forty years old. Did he compose before then, with all trace of his compositions lost? This seems strange. His known songs show him to be a fully proficient, indeed gifted, entertaining, witty poet. Was it the urgent political situation that stimulated him to write? Or did it prompt their circulation, and hence their survival? Whatever the case, he soon (or perhaps had already) gained a reputation for war songs, as the song commissioned by Count Raymond V of Toulouse shows.[47]

His words were powerful, as he and the *rics* were well aware. He could damage reputations as well as stirring men up to war and affect alliances. 'If the count (Richard) treats me well I'll be very useful to him in his affairs,' he says, and if he is not rich enough to travel far to war, he can help through his 'shrewd words'. He found the company of the Plantagenet nobles rewarding and exciting, for their free spending, but also because it both gave him protection and made him feel important and influential. He could present himself as in the know (which he often was), able to share a joke with Richard at the king of France's expense, and was confident enough to tease them both: 'Now I'm afraid of Lord Yes-and-No (Richard),' he says playfully, 'as he doesn't like me to rebuke him in the least, and the French king is being far too sensitive and I'm afraid he will come down on me like a ton of bricks. But I've braved more dukes, princes and emirs in song than were ever at the siege of Troy.'[48] He wore his art lightly, even when he was at his most serious, aligning himself with the traditional playfulness of Occitan courtly life: 'We Limousins will conquer common sense with folly,' he says of the Young King's war against Richard, 'joyfully, for we want people to give gifts and laugh.' Clever with words, he nonchalantly rounds off a contrafactum of Arnaut Daniel's *Lo ferm voler*, with its challenging rhymes, by saying he has 'run out of rhymes in *omba*, *om* or *esta*'.[49]

Bertran's American editor William Paden argues that he composed two songs after his retirement to the Cistercian monastery of Dalon in 1195. This is unsure; their author may have been his son Bertran. Now generally attributed to him is a single religious song, a farewell to the world: 'When I meditate and reflect on who I am and from where I come, I am amazed and cross myself at how long God was willing to suffer my wrongdoings. But may the One Who is true and strong, since it pleases Him that I should turn to Him, deign to kill the sin now that my evil inclination is dead.'[50] He probably died in around 1215.

EIGHT

Raimbaut de Vaqueiras

Of humble origins, Raimbaut was born in the Vaucluse in 1155–60. He began his career as a jongleur but soon became an itinerant troubadour, and by 1177 he was travelling widely across northern Italy.[1] The Malaspina family welcomed him for a few years (1182–5), and by 1182 he had met the marquis Boniface of Montferrat, who was to become his close friend and patron. Raimbaut returned twice to Provence, in 1188–9 and 1195–6, but by 1197 he had settled at the court of Montferrat, eventually following Boniface to the East on the Fourth Crusade. He served him not only as troubadour but as a combatant, and in 1194, after taking part in a military campaign in Sicily, he became the only troubadour of poor origins ever to have been knighted. Raimbaut thanks him in his three-part Epic Letter, composed in Greece in the spring of 1205 after the crusaders had captured Constantinople, when Raimbaut must have been in his mid- to late forties.

Valiant Marquis, lord of Montferrat, I thank God for
granting you such honour that you have conquered
and spent and gifted more than any uncrowned man
of Christendom. I praise God for it, because He has so
advanced me that I have found in you a most kind lord.
You have graciously maintained and equipped me, and
shown me great kindness and from low estate raised me

Raimbaut, historiated initial from *Recueil des poésies des troubadours*, 13th century.

> on high, and from nothing made me a knight of repute, welcomed at court and praised by ladies.[2]

The Epic Letter is our richest source for the troubadour's life. Consisting of three decasyllabic monorhyme *laisses*, it borrows its form from the *chanson de geste* or epic: a choice designed to highlight the troubadour's military services and support requests for a more materially substantial reward than his knighthood.

> I have served you willingly, in good faith, wholeheartedly and gladly, to the utmost of my power. With you I have devised many a courtly stratagem, and have served ladies with you on many a fine occasion, and I have ridden to war with you, and through arms have lost and won, and taken many a blow and with you given many . . . I have helped you to conquer empire and kingdom and these lands and islands and a duchy, and to capture kings and

> princes and a principality, and to vanquish many an armed knight. Many a fortified castle and city, many a splendid palace have I razed with you, and besieged emperor, king and emir, and the Greek commander Lascaris, and the prostrator in the Petrion.

While fighting the communes of Asti, he saved Albert of Malaspina, who had fallen from his horse, suffered dire captivity, protected Boniface at Messina when 'darts and bolts, arrows and javelins, lances and swords and knives and billhooks were hitting [him] in the chest and face,' and was wounded through his armour at the siege of Constantinople.

> If you have not made me very wealthy, it will not seem that I have been by your side and served you in the way of which I have reproachfully reminded you. Yet you know that I speak the whole truth, lord marquis . . . When a loyal vassal serves a good lord, he acquires merit

Conquest of Constantinople, miniature from *Croniques abregies commençans au temps de Herode Antipas* . . ., 15th century.

> from it and receives a good reward in return: so I await recompense and a gift for it, lord marquis.[3]

'Courtly stratagems' feature in the third *laisse*, when Raimbaut reminds his lord of the madcap adventures in their youth. He patently relishes the memory of their close friendship. But has the marquis, now embroiled in grave matters of state,[4] cooled off? The troubadour states that he wants to refresh their bond, 'since it is a grievous thing, my lord, to abandon and forsake a friend, whom one should cherish' (13–14). Slightly apologetic in his evocation of their more frivolous past – 'I'm afraid this might be unbecoming for us, who ought to be teaching others' (3–4) – Raimbaut defends their actions in rescuing young noblewomen from unwanted suitors.

> For the first thing a young nobleman must do is choose whether he wishes to win great glory or to renounce it, as you chose, my lord, who right from the outset desired to raise your worth to such great heights that you made both yourself and me praised everywhere, you as lord and me as a young man. (7–12)

These actions were 'so splendid in a young man they could not be bettered' (5–6): together they had rescued Saldina de Mar from the Marquis of Malaspina to give her to Ponset of Aguilar, 'who lay dying in bed for love of her' (20), and Jacobina of Ventimiglia, who was about to be taken off to Sardinia to be married against her will. Raimbaut plays up the romantic aspects of this escapade, redolent of French chivalric romance:

> You began to sigh a little, and you remembered how she gave you a kiss on taking leave of you, when she begged you so dearly to protect her from her uncle, who sought

> unjustly to deprive her of her inheritance . . . It was I who carried her to the port at the moment of embarkation. The alarm was raised on land and sea, and footmen and horsemen chased after us in hot pursuit; we prepared to leave, and we thought we should cleverly escape them all, when the men of Pisa came to attack us. When we saw so many horsemen ahead in our way, riding in such close order – so many hauberks and fine, glittering helmets, so many banners streaming in the wind – we hid between Albenga and Finale; there we heard many a horn and bugle sounding on many a side, many a warcry being shouted: no need to ask if we were afraid. For two days we stayed without food or drink; and when the third day came and we thought there was no way out, we met twelve thieves in the Belhestar pass who were there to rob. We were in a quandary because it was impossible to fight on horseback. I went forward on foot to engage them, and was wounded by a lance through the gorget, but I wounded three or four of them, I think, so that I made them all turn back . . . Then we joyfully ate a frugal midday meal of bread alone, without drinking or washing. (25–65)

The Letter culminates in praises of his patron's courtly qualities and reinforcement of his own credentials as deserving of reward. Boniface has conducted himself as the ideal lord: he has found high-born husbands for one hundred maidens who would otherwise have had no future; he has remained impervious to flattery, assisting widows and orphans and showing compassion to the unfortunate; and he has used his wealth and power wisely.

> Alexander left to you his generosity, and Roland and the twelve peers their daring, and the gallant Berart lady-service and graceful discourse. Your court is governed by

> all fine manners: munificence and the courting of ladies, elegant dress, handsome armour, trumpets and diversions and viols and song, and it has never pleased you to keep a porter at mealtimes . . . And since, my lord, I know so much of your affairs, you must reward me as for three of the others, and this is just, for in me you may find a witness, a knight and a poet. (100–118)

Events overtook Raimbaut's hopes for a settled future. Boniface died fighting against the Bulgars in 1207, and of our knight-troubadour we hear no more.

Chivalry

Raimbaut's sense of identity is closely bound up with the military life. He stands at an interesting stage in the history of chivalry.[5] Medieval chivalric ideals developed differently in different regions, and 'chivalry' is a protean term. In its fullest form it has been described as an ethos in which martial, aristocratic and Christian elements were fused together, in 'a man of aristocratic standing and probably noble ancestry, who is capable, if called upon, of equipping himself with a war horse and the arms of a heavy cavalryman, and who has been through certain rituals that make him what he is – who has been "dubbed" to knighthood, and who consequentially thinks of himself as belonging to an order of knighthood with a special code of values'.[6] These values may emphasize various ideas, such as martial prowess, vassalic loyalty, courtly manners, courtly love or religious devotion. In the case of courtly love, valiant deeds may be seen as a cause for merit in the lady's eyes and for some form of reward. Courtly love may be viewed as a requisite of the ideal knight, while religious ideas may emphasize the protection of the unarmed (women, children, the clergy), or else God's service on crusade. In this full sense chivalry only seems to have emerged in France and Anglo-Norman England in about 1180, coinciding with the emergence of Old French romances. However, to judge by the literary sources, French ideals of chivalry apparently made relatively little impact on Occitan mentality. Here the knight in Occitania seems above all to have been the old-fashioned, pre-chivalric knight, defined essentially by his professional function and the prestige that went with it. Occitans were less inclined to idealize war than their northern counterparts, particularly after the brutal Albigensian Crusade – hardly the embodiment of chivalric ideals. And there is little sign of southern knights beginning to close themselves off as a caste.

Raimbaut seems to have been a squire in his early service of Boniface, but he was certainly not an apprentice knight: he was of poor birth and knighting was a reward for military service, not part of the progress of a young nobleman.[7] His situation was particular. He moved between Provence and Italy, and it is in Italy where he became a knight. In his Epic Letter he makes no mention of a formal rite by which his knighthood was conferred, though elsewhere he refers in passing to the marquis putting on his sword (XXII, 56).[8] He was first and foremost a knight in its old-fashioned sense of armed horseback warrior – and the practicalities of warfare actually meant that at Constantinople he fought on foot, armed like a Brabantine rather than a knight, proudly and without suggestion of shame.[9] He went on crusade, but his poetry makes no connection between this and God's service: paramount is the service of his earthly lord Boniface. However, it might be said that a Christian element creeps in with the duty of a knight to protect the weak against the strong.[10]

Beyond these aspects his knightly ethos relates to the life of the court, including the service of ladies in general, and courtly love in particular: 'Courts and wars and tournaments and assaults and lady-service and generosity and entertainment are my whole preoccupation.'[11] In French courtly romance a knight's prowess in battle or tournaments is customarily inspired by love, and/or proves his worthiness as a suitor, but the situation in Raimbaut's poems is rather different. In a group of four of his earliest pieces composed in Provence in 1195–6,[12] love and prowess compete rather than complement each other as alternative sources of personal merit. For disappointment in love, Raimbaut declares, the active life is worthy compensation:

> A man can easily have joy and worth
> without love, knowing how to strive for them,
> if he avoids all conduct unbecoming
> and does all good within his power.
> So while I am deprived of love,
> I act and help as best I can,
> and if I lose my lady and love
> I do not wish to lose merit and worth,
> for I can live differently, with honour and valour,
> because I do not care to double my loss.

> Galloping and trotting, jumping and running,
> keeping watch, pain and fatigue
> will henceforth be my leisure,
> and I shall endure cold and heat
> armed with iron and with wood and steel,
> and my lodgings will be woods and paths,
> and my *cansos* will be *sirventes* with *descortz*,
> and I shall support the weak against the strong.[13]

His experiences in Italy colour his return to Provence. An apparently failed attempt to reintegrate himself into the Occitan world – or games – of *fin'amor* lead him to call this concept into question:

> I have no idea why the love that people celebrate so much causes me such distress, or where it can be found, for I have not heard it nor can I see or hear it; but I seem to find in it more injustice than justice. Yet I hear it called *amor fina* by those who invoke it. This is the comfort that vexes and destroys me, and makes me love the one who keeps me close and flees from me, and in fleeing pursues and hunts me down (VI, 1–8).

Of course, all this rhetoric is part of the game of love. But it is interesting that in the midst of his paradoxical protestations he threatens to leave for the region of Tortona and say farewell to Provence and Gap.[14] Italy was where he was knighted, and he carries this identity with him proudly, with its own set of values; when he returns to Provence it is almost as if *fin'amor* is an alien concept.

Back in Montferrat, in his *cansos* his requests for love are more traditionally respectful,[15] but he notably imbues them with the language of warfare:

> I have waged war against love in the same way as the noble vassal wages war on a wicked overlord who wrongly robs him of his land, thus inciting him to war, and when he realizes that his war is profitless he then comes to sue for mercy to regain his rights. I, too, so long to recover joy that I seek to beg pardon from love for its own wrongdoing, and I turn my pride into humility.[16]

Knighthood is even incorporated into his love songs through the androgynous pseudonym he bestows on his lady: Bel Cavalier (Fair Knight); and he pledges to 'shout the noble warcry of her name'.[17]

When he takes part in a *partimen* with Perdigon and Count Ademar II of Poitiers,[18] Raimbaut defends the warrior's way of life. He himself initiates the debate and sets up the rules: which of three barons is best: a lavish spender given to display, a prudent but moderately generous spender, or a hospitable, excellent warrior, who equips his soldiers well? Each participant speaks according to his own interests (as no doubt agreed in advance). Raimbaut defends 'the man who takes pain to equip his own fight men and his mercenaries', while Perdigon dismissively scoffs, 'as for Sir Raimbaut, let him make out a case for the French, whose sole concerns are fighting and drinking wine' (vv. 23–4); 'Sir Raimbaut speaks up for those fat bellies who believe in nothing but eating their fill' (vv. 45–6); 'as for Sir Raimbaut, when he gallops up in his armour he looks much more like a jongleur than a knight' (vv. 55–6). It is interesting that even before the Albigensian Crusade, it is the French who are invoked as representing the knight's way of life, rather than the Italians who have given Raimbaut his knighthood.

Crusades

In August 1201 Boniface was elected leader of the Fourth Crusade. Raimbaut excitedly celebrated the honour shown to his friend and patron.

> Now people can recognise and prove
> that for good deeds God gives a good reward.
> The noble marquis He has recompensed,
> making his reputation soar above the best,
> so that the crusaders of Champagne and of France
> have besought God for him, as best of all
> to recover the holy sepulchre and the cross
> where Jesus was, for he wishes in his company

the honoured marquis, and God has given him the power
of good warriors and of land and wealth
and a noble heart best to do what is fitting for him.

Urging others to follow him in his noble cause, he adopts the language of chivalric epic to rouse crusaders in the East and West to glorious deeds:

May St Nicholas of Bari guide our fleet,
and the men of Champagne raise their standard,
and the marquis cry 'Montferrat and the lion!',
and the Flemish count 'Flanders!' as they give great blows,
and let each there strike with his sword and break his
lance,
and easily we'll kill and smash the Turks to pieces,
and on the battlefield recover the True Cross
which we have lost, and the valiant kings of Spain
gather great hosts for conquering the Moors,
for the marquis is going raise his army and besiege
the sultan, and soon pass through Romagna.[19]

Things did not turn out as planned. After their deviation to Greece and the conquest of Constantinople, the crusaders abandoned any intention of continuing on to the Holy Land and set about establishing themselves as rulers of Frankish Greece, the new Latin empire. There were two contenders for the imperial throne: Boniface and Baldwin of Flanders. Baldwin was elected. The losing contender had been promised all of Asia Minor and the Peloponnese, but what Boniface really wanted was the crown of Thessalonica. A rift developed between the two men and Boniface's wish was put before a council of barons. Our troubadour was deeply disappointed at Baldwin's election and resented his delay in honouring what he saw as his promise to the marquis.

Negotiations were difficult, and the emperor's councillors were urging him to break his promise. Raimbaut used his poetic skills to lobby Baldwin directly and try to bypass the influence of the privy council. His hard-hitting *sirventes* begins by disparaging the emperor's lack of authority over his barons, sarcastically labouring the idea of council, councillors and counsel:

> I offer counsel to the emperor,
> since he conducts all his cases by council,
> and would not do anything more
> or less than his councillors
>   want him to say and do:
> and I counsel him, should he aspire to excellence
> to make gifts without counsel from now on;
> and without his barons' *conseil*, let him
> accept the counsel of the worthiest man;
>   for this is *conseil* fit for an emperor.

Playing on the ambivalence of the word *conseil*, both 'counsel' and 'council', he deftly draws attention to Baldwin's need to behave with honour or risk alienating his allies. The emperor will need both valour and unity in the face of hostile forces on all sides: 'The Vlachs, Cumans and Russians, Turks, Pagans and Persians will be against him, along with the Greeks, and if he does not suffer the burden for glory, he may undo everything he has done.' He also plays on the crusaders' spiritual anxieties over their guilt at sacking Christian cities and religious foundations, which can only be justified if they do not forget their ultimate goal of taking the crusade on to Africa and the Holy Land:

> For he and we are all sinners
> from burning monasteries and palaces,
> wherein I see clergy and laymen sinning;

and if he does not aid the sepulchre,
    and the conquest makes no progress,
our sin against God will be greater,
for the pardon will turn to sin.

He fearlessly names the main players in this decision-making, conceding that the seneschal Thierry of Los and the poet and diplomat Conon de Béthune – with whom he otherwise had good relations and on a later occasion exchanged a *tenso*[20] – may be irritated by his intervention, and appealing directly to the leader, diplomat and chronicler Geoffrey of Villehardouin and Milon of Brabant as possible supporters of his cause. The dispute was settled in Boniface's favour, apparently in just the way the troubadour had advocated.

For whatever reason, he did not accompany his patron on his last campaign. Remaining in Thessalonica, he looks back in song at a lost time of love and courtly pleasures, and the skirmishes of siege warfare bring him no consolation. In what seems a self-conscious effort to make the best of a grim situation, he wistfully imbues the crusade with epic qualities, reminding himself and his listeners of their achievements, which surpass those of legendary heroes:

Alexander and Charlemagne
and king Louis never undertook
an expedition so honourable, nor would
the brave lord Aimeri or Roland with his warriors
have ever been able so nobly to conquer
such a powerful empire by force
as we have won, whereby our faith mounts high;
for we have made emperors and dukes
and kings, and we have fortified castles
close to the Turks and to the Arabs,

and opened up the highways and the ports
from Brindisi to St George's Straits.

By us Damascus will be attacked,
and Jerusalem will be conquered,
and the realm of Syria liberated:
for the Turks find this in their prophecies.[21]

But it ends on a bitter, ominous note, denouncing the thousands of armed crusaders who had newly arrived in the port of Constantinople, then almost defenceless. On hearing of the Latins' disastrous defeat at Adrianople, and despite the desperate pleas of military and religious leaders, they had fled in panic.

Innovations and genres

Raimbaut's lyric legacy is a collection of remarkably vivid, witty, diverse and innovative songs. Many draw on popularizing elements. Their genres include *cansos*, *sirventes*, *tensos* and *partimens*, *descorts* ('discords', possibly the earliest examples of the genre),[22] a *devinalh* (riddle poem),[23] an *estampida*, two satirical tournaments, inspired by a genre of northern French origin, entitled *Garlambey* and *Carros*, and possibly an *alba* and a popularizing song in a woman's voice inspired by Galego-Portuguese *cantigas de amigo*.[24] The first of the 'tournaments' stages mock-heroic jousts sung to the tune of an epic poem, with obscene undertones, in which named riders compete and exchange mounts (their own wives and lovers).

The lord of Baux
    made a good start,
but to tell the truth,
    his horse had a

big mouth and a fat belly
  and seemed bad-tempered,
so that that day the warrior's
  seat was precarious.
Sir Raimon Rainouart
  immediately knocked him
onto the rushes with his lance
  and locked up the horse,
but Sir Guilhem apparently
  unperturbed
sought compensation elsewhere.[25]

The *Carros*, a battle of women, is set at the court of Montferrat. Glorifying Boniface's daughter Beatrice, it simultaneously satirizes the autonomous Italian towns or communes of Piedmont and Lombardy that were threatening the feudal power her father represented.[26] As she triumphs over an army of Italian noblewomen, their names deprecatingly signal his enemies. The most striking feature of their campaign, typical of the communes of the time, is a *carros* or war-chariot, mounted by citizens armed with distinctly un-knightly pigskin cuirasses, jerkins, bows and quivers.

One of Raimbaut's greatest lyric innovations is the use of multilingualism. In one *descort* (XVI), the pretext of being distraught over love prompts him to compose a 'discord on love': because his lady's heart has changed, he will produce 'discordance in the rhymes, melodies and languages'. The melodies have not survived, but they must have changed along with the rhymes and languages, which switch from one stanza to the next: Provençal, Italian, French, Gascon and Galego-Portuguese, with two lines each in the *tornada*. The other multilingual piece is a *tenso* between the poet and a Genoese woman who addresses him disparagingly in her own tongue as a mere minstrel or *Jujar*.

In their comical exchange the troubadour begins by wooing her in courtly tones while she rebuffs him in round and vulgar terms, and ends with the ribaldry typical of Guilhem IX's burlesque: 'I shall beseech you to allow me to give you a go, in the way a Provençal does it when he's mounted' (III, 87–90). Although attempts have been made to identify the Genoese woman as a *trobairitz*, she is Raimbaut's invention. The 'thrust' of the song is political: a comic clash of cultures, courtly in the case of the troubadour and his aristocratic patrons, mercantile in that of their rivals in the Genoese republic. As Gilda Caïti-Russo concludes,

> We are faced with linguistic and, naturally, cultural imperialism, where Provençal imposes itself as the dominant language, in a new politico-cultural diglossia that contrasts the speech of the communes with a court language made their own by the vassals of the Empire, such as the Malaspinas and then above all the Montferratos.[27]

The Genoese woman reappears in a *tenso* with the marquis Albert Malaspina (IV), who begins by vilifying Raimbaut's love-life and *domna*:

> Now tell me, Raimbaut, if it pleases you,
> whether it has befallen you as I hear tell:
> that your lady from Tortona here, for whom
> you have composed so many futile love songs,
> has conducted herself badly towards you,
> since she has made such a *sirventes* about you
> that you are dishonoured and that she is shamed,
> saying your love brings her no honour or profit,
> which is why she has distanced herself from you.[28]

During the course of the exchange, where the poet plays briefly on the idea of *amor de lonh* (v. 9), the two interlocutors bombard each other with insults. Albert sneers at the troubadour's earlier life of wandering on foot like a miserable jongleur, 'poor in worldly goods and unlucky in love', and his present failure, now that he has a charger, to 'strike a blow with sword or lance', and ends by calling him a 'scabby wether-face, fat-paunch!' In turn Raimbaut berates the marquis for greed and faith-breaking, speaking 'vexatious, churlish things' and being even better at doing them, living a life of treachery and guile, yet failing in his military and political enterprises. The *tenso* belongs to the medieval poetics of insult. It is a joke, immersed in the troubadour culture of *foudat gaia*, and the existence of the *domna* of Tortona is part of it.[29]

Raimbaut's *Kalenda maia*, an *estampida*, adds a dance song to his poetic repertoire. The surviving melody and verse form point to a marked stamping rhythm, in accordance with the term's etymology, more or less incorporated into modern performances on YouTube. While it addresses Raimbaut's courtly lady *Bel Cavalier*, the dance element, the fact that this is a May song and its emphasis on the 'jealous one' point to popular tradition. The versification is highly demanding, each stanza containing only three rhymes in twenty lines (or part-lines, depending on how the poem is set out on the page) of an average of three and a half syllables.

Kalenda maia
ni fueils de faia
ni chans d'auzell   ni flors de glaia
non es qe·m plaia,
pros dona gaia,
tro qu'un isnell   messagier aia
del vostre bell   cors, qi·m retraia

plazer novell q'amors atraia
e jaia
e·m traia
vas vos donna veraia
e chaia
de plaia
·l gelos, anz qe·m n'estraia.[30]

> There is no May Day or leaf of beech or birdsong or gladiolus flower that can please me, noble merry lady, until I have a swift messenger from your lovely person, telling me of some new delight that love and joy may bring me and draw me to you, true lady, and may the jealous one fall wounded before I withdraw from there.

There is a tight connection between text and music, the hammering rhythm that coincides with the stress of the very short lines.[31] The *razo* states that the troubadour composed it at the court of Montferrat, inspired by the tune of an *estampie* played on the vielle by a passing French jongleur. As the French *estampie* was a purely musical genre and the oldest French *estampies* with text date only from the fourteenth century, *Kalenda maia* would seem to offer yet more evidence of Raimbaut's originality in setting such dance music to words.

NINE

Folquet de Marselha

Folquet has a double identity. For about twenty years he was a troubadour, known by the diminutive form of his name. He then abandoned the secular world to enter the Church, eventually becoming Bishop Fulk of Toulouse. In this capacity he continued to be important for the story of the troubadours, for he played a key role supporting the Albigensian Crusade, the Church-sanctioned invasion of the south of modern-day France by the French under Simon de Montfort, which provoked passionate responses from other troubadours and induced many to leave their homeland for Italy or Iberia.

His *vida* relates that he was from Marseille, the son of a Genoese merchant named Anfos who on his death left him very wealthy: he sought after merit and worth, serving notable barons and other men, mixing with them, dispensing gifts and 'coming and going'.[1] It claims he was welcomed by Richard the Lionheart, Count Raymond of Toulouse and Barral, Viscount of Marseille; that he composed love songs complaining of unrequited love for Barral's wife; and that it was after the death of all these that he abandoned the world and entered the Cistercian order with his wife and two children, to become abbot of the rich abbey of Thoronet and then bishop of Toulouse, where he died.

The *vida* was probably originally composed while he was still alive, and is relatively well-informed. Other evidence confirms that he was son of a merchant in Marseille and that he was

Thoronet Abbey, built between 1160 and 1230.

married with two sons, Anfos and Peire, who entered the Cistercian monastery of Grandselve. It is credible but unproven that his father came from the rich trading port of Genoa, and that Folquet was, or became, a wealthy man. What happened to his wife is unknown but John of Garland, who taught at the university of Toulouse, described him as a man 'renowned on account of his spouse, his progeny and his home'. Folquet did complain of unrequited love in *cansos* addressed to Barral's wife, and he did have contact with Richard, though there is no evidence to support the *vida*'s explanation for Folquet's decision to enter the Church. That he was a monk and abbot at Thoronet is likely but uncertain.[2] He was probably born in about 1150; he became a bishop in 1205, and died on Christmas Day 1231.[3]

Dante praises him both as a troubadour and as a cleric. In the *De vulgari eloquentia* he cites his *Tant m'abellis l'amoros pessamens*

(II), alongside Arnaut Daniel's *Sols sui qui sai lo sobrafan qe.m sortz*, as an example of excellent construction, and he celebrates him in Canto IX of *Paradiso* for his pastoral and political activities against the Cathar heretics.[4] He had no small resonance as a troubadour: elements of his songs find echoes in poets from Occitania, northern France, Catalonia, Italy and Germany.[5]

Folquet the troubadour

Folquet's surviving works span a period of about twenty years.[6] Mainly comprising *cansos*, they also include a *partimen*, a joglaresc-style *cobla*, some three songs involving crusade themes, a *planh*, a religious *alba* and a penitential piece. He did not compose from financial need;[7] indeed, if the *vida* is to be believed, it was he who dispensed largesse. For this affluent bourgeois, courtly song was a passport to social mobility. It gave him entry into the courts of Alfonso II of Aragon and Richard the Lionheart, both of whom invited him to sing for them, and to those of Count Ramón Berenguer IV of Provence, the viscounts of Marseille, Millau and Nîmes, the lord of Montpellier William VIII, and other greater or lesser lords of the last quarter of the twelfth century. Some of these, such as Bertran de Born and Raimon de Miraval, were troubadours themselves.[8] Other troubadours with whom he enjoyed personal contact included Pons de Capdoill, Peire Vidal and the Monk of Montaudon.[9]

Love

The majority of his songs are *cansos*. Their themes are conventional, dwelling, as Nicole Schulman has observed, on the issue of the obligation and proper behaviour between lover and beloved, and hopes of *merce* (pity). 'Unlike some troubadours, Folc's romantic hopes are rather subdued. All he seeks

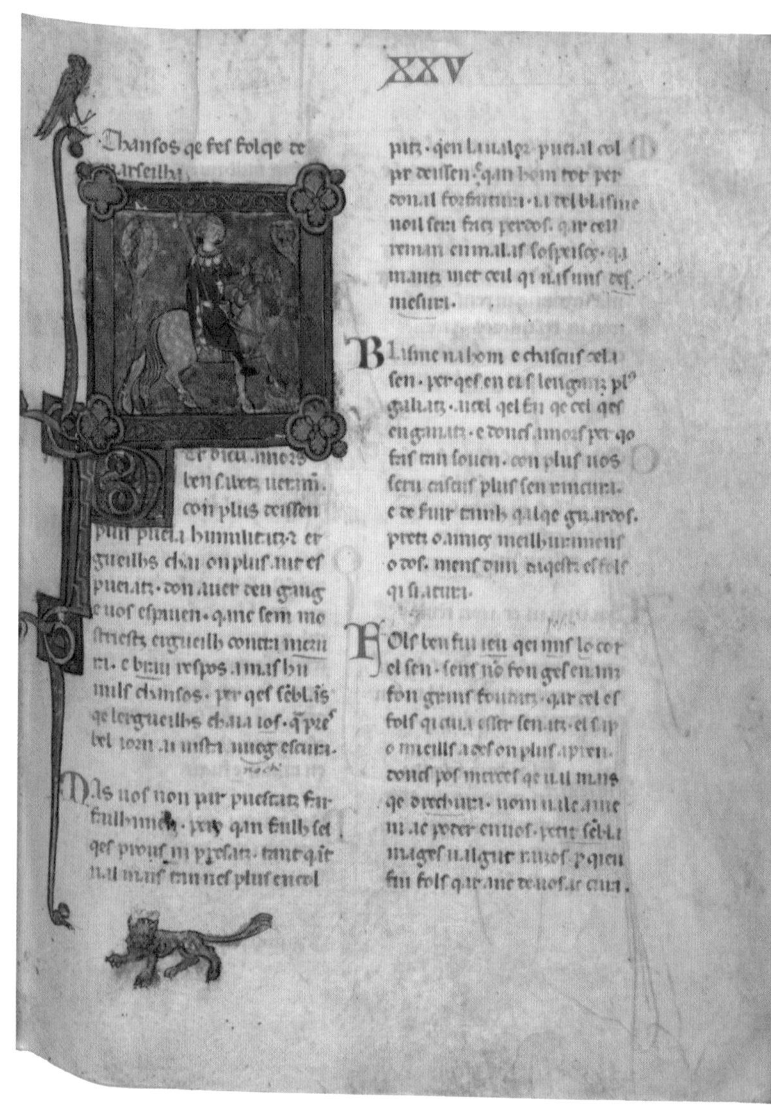

Fulk of Toulouse as a troubadour, miniature from a *Chansonnier provençal* manuscript, 14th century.

is toleration, that his beloved should allow him to sing for her.'[10] Although this conventionality is less to the taste of modern readers than the lively originality of many other troubadours, some studies have brought out both the complex formal structure of his words, as Dante already emphasized, and the excellence of his music.[11] Here is the first stanza of his only song that Dante cites:

Tant m'abellis l'amoros pessamens
que s'es vengutz e mon fin cor assire,
per que no.i pot nuills autre pens caber
ni mais negus no m'es doutz ni plazens,
c'adoncs viu sas quan m'aucio'ill cossire;
e fin'amors aleuja mo martire
que.m promet joi mas trop lo.m dona len,
c'ab bel semblan m'a trainat longamen. (II, 1–8)

So lovely to me is the amorous reflection
which comes to settle in my faithful heart,
through which no other thought can find a place in it,
and none is e'er so sweet and pleasing for me,
that now I live in health when I am slain by care,
and perfect love alleviates my anguish,
plighting me joy but granting it too slowly,
for with fair semblance long has it made me languish.

The long-drawn-out trisyllables of the first line, the hypotactic single-sentence stanza, words evoking slowness (*len*) and lingering (*trainat*), gradually leading to the final trisyllabic *longamen*, slow the pace and induce the listener to pause on each element. Words evoking reflectiveness and thought (*pessamens*, *pen*), impregnated with the vocabulary of sweetness, pleasure, life and joy (*doutz*, *plazens*, *viu*, *joi*), interweave with oxymoronic expressions of unrequited love-longing: *amoros pessamens* (*pessamens* means 'care', sorrow' as well as 'thought'), *sas/cossire* (healthy/care), *amors/martire/joi* ('love'/'anguish' or 'martyrdom'), reinforced by the ambiguity of *bel semblan* (a lovely face, or the lady's welcoming expression, or love's fair or deceiving appearance). Conventional, yes: but an eloquent distillation of courtly love.[12]

A *partimen* about love is a typical way for a troubadour to integrate himself into courtly society, and Folquet engages in one of these with the troubadour Tostemps, almost certainly the minor lord Raimon de Miraval. Folquet proposes the topic.

> Tostemps, if you are an expert on love, choose which of two ladies is preferable if you are a lover: one who is not devious towards you and tolerates no other admirer, yet she never reveals to you that she loves you or is favourably inclined towards you; or another who loves you as much but has one or two other lovers, granted that she brings you as many joys as a true love ought to bring.[13]

Tostemps chooses to defend the lady who keeps her love secret without betraying him with 'fair joys' (presumably dallying with other suitors), which obliges Folquet to side with the one free with her favours to the lover 'even if she does go running around once you are away'. Tostemps dismisses the defence of a lady whose worth is 'never again pure or unsullied', while Folquet ripostes that it is 'better to put up with agreeable deceit, for this is just one of those betrayals that many men have to endure'. The verbal joust is a game, but one can see how, once he entered the Church, the former troubadour could have felt embarrassed about it, especially as he had been a married man. This latter state was clearly not a problem within a courtly environment, especially since his love songs had always implied that any love on his part was unrequited, and moreover *cansos* were an artistic creation embodying the secular values of the court. For a bishop things were very different.

Crusade songs and farewell to the worldly life

Crusading themes figure in three of Folquet's songs of secure attribution. Was he was already a monk when he composed songs on crusading themes? The earliest of the three, *Ai! quan gen vens et ab quan pauc d'afan* (VI), dates from the time of the Third Crusade, in 1190. When Richard the Lionheart, much blamed for delaying his departure for the Holy Land, finally arrived in Marseille to await his fleet, Folquet composed a song at his request. Like many songs of the period it begins with love themes, which suggest that this is a conventional piece of courtly entertainment, and switches after a few stanzas to topical matters, in this case praise of Richard's commitment to his crusading vow. Because of the love elements it seems unlikely that the troubadour has yet abandoned the world of the court. Five years later, this is less clear. *Oimais no·i conosc razo* (XVIII) exhorts people to take the cross to fight in Spain alongside the king of Aragon, and *Chantars mi torna ad afan* (XIV), dated to the period between April and July 1195, urges Richard and Philip Augustus to follow the example of Emperor Henry VI, who had vowed to depart on a fresh expedition to the Holy Land. Recalling the death of his patron Barral, Folquet declares that people are pressuring him to produce a song:

> Singing becomes painful for me when I remember Sir Barral, and since I care no more about love, I do not know how or of what to sing; but everyone is asking for a song and they do not care about the topic: so I need to make it anew, with the words and the melody; and since without love I am forced to sing through a debt of folly, my song

> will be excellent even if it is neither bad nor good. (xiv, 1–12)

It is interesting that Folquet claims to be 'without love', and to be looking for a new topic. He goes on to identify love with greed, and treat them both as soul-destroying.

> Lovers are all the same, and likewise the greedy rich, for with searing pain they constantly diminish their joy the more they have of it: they are like a window that grows smaller if it is leaned against; the more a man captures what he is hunting, the more he is motivated to pursue the hunt; so I consider as better than a king or an emperor the man who vanquishes both of those bad qualities which vanquish most of the barons.
>
> It would be good if people valued God as much as themselves, and goodness as much as wickedness! But people value what is worthless and consider their advantage as harm; so I do not dare speak in song of what is to your advantage, for this does not please the world, nor do I believe it will like anyone who tells it of anything that is to their detriment; but yet I can speak of the dishonour if the Turks are conquered or brought low by each other, since all the conquered conquer us. (13–36)

The dating of Folquet's 'conversion' is difficult to resolve,[14] but it seems that while he is still in demand as a troubadour, this song shows him wrestling to reconcile his moral and religious leanings with the secular life. This was at a time of great spiritual upheaval following the loss of Jerusalem, the True Cross and the holy places, and it would not be surprising if the changing mood of the times contributed to his change of heart.

A song of penitence is attributed to Folquet in manuscript R. In the only other manuscript, a Catalanized version, it is anonymous. Paolo Squillacioti sees no reason to reject the attribution, which other scholars previously considered doubtful.[15] Comprising 148 octosyllabic couplets followed by *Amen*, it begins:

> Lord God, who made Adam,
> and tested the faith of Abraham,
> and deigned to take on flesh and blood
> for us in Your great loving-kindness,
> then yielded up Your body to martyrdom,
> in which respect I, on reflection, consider
> that You acted with extraordinary humility
> given Your high power;
> God, Jesus Christ, son of Mary,
> Lord, show me the right way
> and disregard my faults,
> and turn me back to the paths of righteousness.
> Now it is fitting for me to lay myself bare,
> so long have I dwelled in evil works.
> I always loved great avarice
> and had my heart set on covetousness;
> I liked accumulating things for myself,
> and not always wholly in good faith;
> I eagerly amassed another's property,
> taking no heed of what or whose it was,
> and was full of ill-will
> and supported work of the devil –
> until it came to me that I should cease all this
> and serve You, true God. (XXVII, 1–24)

It certainly seems an appropriate song of a man who turned his back on the world to enter a monastery.

The Cathars and the Albigensian Crusade

In 1208 Occitania faced a crusade on its own Christian soil. Heresy, especially Catharism, was rife here. The Church had made several attempts to counter the threat to its authority by sending preaching missions to the region. The murder of the papal legate Peire de Castelnau, connived at, some thought, by Raymond VI of Toulouse, finally spurred Pope Innocent III to launch a military invasion. Led by the minor French nobleman

Albigensian Crusade, miniature from the *Grandes chroniques de France*, 14th century.

Simon de Montfort, it very quickly turned into a war of French conquest.

Catharism was one of many outcomes of popular spiritual movements advocating a return to the apostolic way of life. Sometimes these movements led to the creation of new monastic orders or other religious enterprises embraced by the established Church. At other times they proved a serious threat to the

Church's hierarchical authority and disciplinary powers in matters of faith when it found itself explicitly or implicitly accused of corruption and worldliness. Catharism used to be thought to have derived from fourth-century Manicheism and, ultimately, the Gnosticism of the early Christians. Historians now generally think it arose from a combination of the indigenous development of contemporary conditions in the West and Bogomil ideas imported by missionaries, merchants or crusaders from the Balkans. Records attest its appearance in Western Europe in the 1140s, though heretics were denounced by Pope Calixtus II, apparently with the support of Guilhem IX, as early as 1119. In 1174–8 the magnitude of the threat can be judged by a meeting held at Saint-Félix-de-Caraman in the Lauragais, which established Cathar bishops for dioceses in France, Toulouse, Carcassonne (which included the whole of Catalonia), Albi, Agen and Lombardy, joining the seven existing churches of Asia.

Very few genuinely Cathar documents survive, and our knowledge of the Cathars and their beliefs has been almost wholly filtered through the records produced by their enemies. But most historians tend to agree that the Cathar elite differed from heretics of other sects in their dualistic beliefs. They believed that the visible world had been created by the Devil or Evil principle, who corresponded to God of the Old Testament.

> Cathar dualism took two main forms known as absolute and mitigated dualism. Absolute dualism admitted two principles, of Good and Evil, which co-exist throughout eternity. It held that Lucifer, son of the Evil principle, had secretly entered the domain of the God of Good and succeeded in seducing certain angels. After being expelled from heaven the souls of the angels became imprisoned in earthbound, material bodies. Through reincarnation they passed from one material body to another until, by means

> of the ritual of *consolamentum*, they could be freed to re-enter heaven. Mitigated dualists believed that the Evil principle was an evil angel who would be destroyed at the end of the material world.[16]

Cathars believed they were the true Church of God, the Church of Rome having been created by the world, and therefore the Devil. They therefore rejected its institutions, authority and sacraments, along with the Old Testament God, Law, patriarchs and prophets, and the doctrine of the Incarnation: Jesus was pure spirit, uncontaminated by evil matter, the Virgin Mary being a symbol of the Church, or a woman through whom Christ simply passed in order to appear in spiritual form on earth. They contrasted baptism of the Holy Spirit, or the *consolamentum*, to the baptism by water of the Roman Church, and granted it to believers only, so not usually to children. The person seeking baptism underwent a period of instruction and tests of doctrine and ascetic discipline, and after the ceremony became a 'Perfect', freed from the contamination of evil and able in turn to baptize others. In theory the ritual could not be repeated, so it was important that a Perfect should not lapse into fleshly indulgence and thought of sin; as a consequence most believers only received the *consolamentum* at the end of their lives. A rare practice was the *endura*: a person consoled on their deathbed might not wish to risk recovery and refused further food. Perfects, men or women, were supposed to eschew all physical contact with the opposite sex, and ate no product of sexual generation such as meat, milk, eggs or cheese (fish, being thought to generate spontaneously in water, were excluded from this prohibition). They fasted on certain days of the week and for three forty-day periods during the year, and before times of persecution wore a characteristic black robe, afterwards replaced by a black thread worn next to the skin. Most Cathars were simple believers or *credentes*.

They were not obliged to live the austere lives of the Perfects, whom they supported with gifts of food and clothing, lodging and shelter, and guided from place to place during their persecution. They practised a ritual greeting known as the *meliorametum*: a repeated bow, a request for blessing and a prayer that they might 'make a good end', in other words receive the *consolamentum* before death.

Various ideas have been advanced as to why the south was particularly susceptible to the Cathar heresy. Whatever the case, one of the difficulties of persuading the local rulers to uproot it was that heretics had been raised with them, were members of their families and were seen to live honestly.[17]

As the northern army marched south, the arrival of the crusaders inaugurated an era of summary executions, hitherto unknown in Occitania. In 1209 its siege of Béziers ended with the massacre of its inhabitants. Carcassonne swiftly capitulated. At Castres Simon de Montfort personally supervised the burning of the first Cathar Perfect. After the capture of Minerve the following year, 140 Perfects were burned alive, as were a further three hundred at Lavaur where Dame Giraude, known for her kindness, was thrown down a well and stones heaped upon her. To quote Jonathan Sumption, 'the survivors fled before Simon's soldiers like fieldmice before the reapers into an ever-dwindling corner of tall grass.'[18]

The southern lords began to join together in resistance with the help of Peter II of Aragon, but the battle of Muret in 1213 saw Peter dead and the counts of Toulouse and Foix flee to English territory. At the Lateran Council of 1215 the Occitan lords agreed to persecute heresy, but the arrival of the young Raymond VII in Toulouse in 1216 fired up resistance to the invaders, and Raymond was joyously welcomed into Beaucaire. Montfort besieged it unsuccessfully, then made his way to Toulouse, where he inflicted reprisals on the city, suppressed a rebellion, imposed forced taxes and demolished the fortifications. Raymond VI returned from exile in Spain and entered Toulouse, from which the Toulousains ejected the crusaders; two sieges followed Simon's return. In 1218, before the city walls, he was killed by a piece of heavy masonry fired by women from a trebuchet. Prince Louis of France then marched south and massacred the inhabitants of Marmande, but his venture was unsuccessful, and by 1220 heretics worshipped freely again; Innocent III was dead, Raymond VI died in 1222 and his son Raymond VII had better record of orthodoxy. But in 1226 Louis, now king of France, invaded the Languedoc once more, and he achieved his ends. In 1229 Raymond VII signed the Treaty of Meaux, performing humiliating penance, agreeing to pay indemnity and heavy tribute for five years, and marrying his daughter and heiress Jeanne to the king's brother Alphonse of Poitiers. On Raymond's death his lands were absorbed directly into the French crown.

Fulk's role in the crusade

What was the bishop's role in all this turmoil? What prompted Folquet the troubadour to turn his back on troubadour activities, family and worldly life? An educated man, necessarily educated by the Church, was he troubled by growth of heresy? The details of his decision are hazy.[19] What we do know is that three years before the launch of the crusade, he was elected to the episcopal see of Toulouse, after what is likely to have been a few years as a monk and then an abbot. Schulman estimates that the Cistercians, who had been at the forefront of attempts to extirpate heresy in the south, probably helped to arrange his nomination. In 1198, working together with the pope, this Order adopted a policy of episcopal 'cleansing', replacing many of the southern bishops who had proved ineffective against the heretics.[20] Whatever the truth of his 'conversion', as the new bishop of

Toulouse he was to play a critical role in the crusade, as either supporter or protagonist.

In such a contentious context it is hard to be objective about this man, seen by some as a saint and others as the Antichrist. Of the medieval commentators on the crusaders' side, the most uncompromising was the Cistercian Pierre des Vaux-de-Cernay. This French monk visited the Albigeois in 1212 and 1214, and claims to have written as an eyewitness or to have used only unimpeachable sources. Zealously hostile to the south, he depicts Fulk as a saintly hero standing up to the tyrannical count of Toulouse:

> The tyrant became furious; he sent a knight to the Bishop, ordering him on pain of death to leave the city and all the Count's domains. It is said that on hearing this the Bishop, speaking fervently and fearlessly and with a joyous countenance, answered the knight thus: 'The Count of Toulouse did not make me Bishop, not was I ordained by his hands or on his behalf. It was the humility of the Church that brought about my election, not the power of princes. I will not go on his account. Let him come if he dares. I am ready to embrace the sword if I can attain glory by drinking the cup of suffering. Let the tyrant come, surrounded by knights and armed; he will find me alone and unarmed . . .' What firmness of heart, what marvellous strength of mind! So the fearless servant of God stayed his ground.[21]

William of Puylaurens, who seems to have been in Fulk's entourage during 1228–30, and who recounts episodes about which Fulk had told him in person, takes a more balanced approach, blaming the spread of heresy on the sins of the people but also the laxity of the southern clergy. Despite seeing the crusade as entirely justified, he expresses some sympathy for the people's suffering, and shows some understanding of the Toulousains' grievances against the occupying forces, as the citizens 'refused to submit to masters whose rule was overweening and took refuge in a form of disobedience. They bore with difficulty the yoke which undermined the liberty to which they were accustomed.' But he has nothing but praise for Fulk, whom he calls 'a venerable and pious man', and lauds his generosity to his prelates and to beggars. The editors of his chronicle observe that 'Fulk obviously made a great impression on William and parts of his Chronicle verge on a panegyric of the Bishop.'[22]

Guilhem de Tudela, who between 1210 and 1213 wrote the first part of the Occitan *Song of the Albigensian Crusade*, was originally from Navarre but became a member of the Occitan clergy. He describes Fulk as one unequalled in goodness, whose indefatigable preaching in the Toulousain met with mocking boredom: 'Now the bee's buzzing around!' Guilhem writes that he is 'not surprised [the southerners] are being destroyed, or pillaged, or stripped of their belongings, or violently chastised'. But he is not entirely unsympathetic to their sufferings: at Lavaur he comments that the murder of Dame Giraude 'was a sorrow and a sin, for no man in the world, you can be certain, would ever leave her before being given food'. If the people suffered so much, he concludes regretfully, it was because they did not do what the clergy and the crusaders told them to do.[23]

In the second part of the *Song*, a very different Fulk emerges. Its anonymous author defends the southern cause with intense passion, and for him, Fulk is the Antichrist, only too ready to sanction the pillage and burning of Toulouse:[24] a skilful, manipulative speaker, implacably hostile to the Count of Toulouse and the interests of its citizens, and ruthlessly prepared to break his word. Two episodes stand out. At the time of the Lateran Council he is the spokesman of the Montfort party, and when

Fulk of Toulouse as bishop, historiated initial from a *Chansonnier provençal* manuscript, 13th century.

the crusading army turns back towards Toulouse after its defeat at Beaucaire, he tricks the Toulousains into submission. Here, from high up on a watchtower, he preaches to the people in honeyed, theatrical tones:

> sighing he preaches, with the semblance of tears. 'My Lords,' [he] says, 'I feel great pain in my heart because I can see you are suffering and deeply troubled. I pray to Jesus Christ Whom I worship with a true heart that he purge you of the evil sap and unhealthy humour in you, and give you a positive attitude and restore in you a disposition such that there should be kind affection between you and the count [Simon]. Since God has chosen me as master and doctor and given me as shepherd to His sheep, if they are willing to believe me and not run away, I will defend them from the wolf and the evil robber . . . If I led you to your destruction

> and deceived you . . . Jesus Christ would consider me a deceitful fraud. I would willingly have wild beasts and vultures devour all my flesh and blood, all my force and strength, as long as you are not ill-treated or wretched in any way . . . I beg you to give me the power and grant me the honour of establishing peace and love between you and the count, without any harm coming to your goods, land or persons. Put yourselves in his power without any fear.'[25]

Once they are in the presence of the count, 'play-acting, tears and promises are over. The mask falls, the real Fulk speaks.' He tells the count to take hostages immediately, under his guidance as to which ones best to choose.

> 'I am going to show you how to become master of the Toulousains: I have received them mercifully so that you can take them by surprise. If anyone blames you for having broken my guarantee, justify yourself as best you can, by saying that you are excluding them from my protection, the Church and mercy.'[26]

Gouiran shows how the Anonymous not only emphasizes what he sees as Fulk's profound hypocrisy but depicts him in such a way as to wound him in his most sensitive spot: his former life as a troubadour. In a well-known anecdote Robert de Sorbon relates that 'whenever Folquet, bishop of Toulouse, heard a song he had composed during the time when he lived among lay people, he would put himself on bread and water for the rest of the day.'[27] Earlier the Anonymous actually refers to him as a jongleur rather than a troubadour, putting these lines into the mouth of the Count of Foix:

> With his lying songs and his insinuating words which lead to perdition all those who sing or recite them, with his honed and polished repartees, with our gifts which have made a jongleur out of him, with his bad doctrine, he has become so rich that no-one dares defend what he opposes.[28]

Gouiran comments that this way of demoting him from troubadour to jongleur is a powerful way of discrediting the bishop/troubadour. His speech, with its histrionic gestures and overblown manner, is more like that of a lowly jongleur than of a refined troubadour, and the Anonymous

> is careful never to lose sight of the accusation that is most hurtful to Fulk/Folquet, the one that most lowers him in the estimation of his own people, even more than in those of his adversaries: his behaviour as a *jongleur*. After first denouncing him through the mouth of Raymond-Roger, he takes advantage of the fact that preaching is also clearly a sort of theatre (how could a preacher avoid drawing on an actor's resources?) to reduce this 'performance' to a performance of indignity. It is no bishop who could evoke the wounded and the dead of Montgey by means of grand gesticulations, with the coarseness of a quasi-culinary vocabulary . . . He is a histrionic ham, perfectly capable of cold-bloodedly weeping and ranting before pointing out to Montfort which members of the audience he can incarcerate as he pleases, despite all the most holy guarantees he has given them. At the same time, the pejorative notion of jongleur marks him with the suspicion of *avaritia*.[29]

In modern times, many still see him as an odious figure. But he was also a complex one: 'a multifaceted man who lived in complicated times'.[30] His editor Stanislaw Stronński describes him as a man of superior intelligence and prodigious energy, a crusade leader and preacher charged with important diplomatic missions, convinced of the need for a crusade to extirpate heresy appearing to present grave danger to the Church and society, whose support for Simon de Montfort made him complicit in the acts of cruelty and injustice committed under the pretext of crusading.[31]

Afterword

This book has told the story of some individuals – so many omissions! – remarkable for their brilliant craftsmanship, their emotional power, their new ways of love, their perceptions of war and chivalry, and, finally, the embodiment of a turning point in their history. The Albigensian Crusade, the Church's establishment of the Inquisition and the rising of French power in the south incited a number of troubadours to seek their fortunes in Italy and Iberia. Courts here were already receptive to their language and cultural baggage from visits by earlier composers, and troubadour influence spread into the Sicilian school of poetry at the court of Emperor Frederick II (1220–1250), the *Dolce stil novo* and Dante in Italy, and Galego-Portuguese poetry exemplified by the *Cantigas de Santa María* of Alfonso X of Castile (1252–1284).[1] One of the most interesting troubadours was the Catalan Cerverí de Gerona, who composed in Occitan from 1267 to 1285, at the court of Peter II the Great of Aragon. Miriam Cabré has shown how his 'vast corpus (119 items) acts as a window onto the cultural trends of the thirteenth century' which 'resulted in a renewed troubadour tradition, and coloured its eventual transformation into new schools'.[2]

Meanwhile troubadour songs continued to flourish in the Midi. Indeed, the 'formation of a persecuting society' provoked vigorous satires against clerical greed and hypocrisy by troubadours such as Peire Cardenal and Guilhem Figueira,[3] as well as some rousing political *sirventes* in support of resistance movements against the French during the later stages of the Albigensian wars (1224–33) and, beyond the Pyrenees, the 'Aragonese crusade' of 1283.[4] The Eastern crusades and international conflicts between Church and Empire inspired *sirventes* throughout the thirteenth century.[5] Guiraut Riquier, despite his pessimistic outlook and a feeling of having been 'born too late', found patronage not only in Castile but in Narbonne and Rodez.[6] The court of Provence continued to attract troubadours during the rule of Charles I of Anjou (1246–85), a French ruler imposed as a consequence of the Albigensian wars. He was not much liked and seems to have had little personal interest in their poetry,[7] but troubadours such as Bertran d'Alamanon and the Italian Sordel served him as bureaucrats while maintaining their poetic activities, and were not afraid to criticize or mock him.[8]

REFERENCES

Abbreviations

BSC	Jean Boutière, Alexander H. Schutz and Irénée-Marcel Cluzel, *Biographies des troubadours* (Paris, 1973)
Dizionario	Saverio Guida and Gerardo Larghi, *Dizionario biografici dei trovatori* (Modena, 2013)
DOM	*Dictionnaire de l'occitan médiéval*, www.dom-en-ligne.de
DVE	Dante, *De vulgari eloquentia*, ed. Steven Botterill (Cambridge, 2009)
LR	François-Just-Marie Raynouard, *Lexique roman*, 6 vols (Paris, 1836–44)
LT	*Lecturae tropatorum*, www.lt.unina.it
Rialto	*Repertorio informatizzato dell'antica letteratura trobadorica e occitana*, rialto.unina.it
TB	*Jaufre Rudel: Prince, Amant et poète. Trobada tenue à Blaye les 24 et 25 juin 2011*, ed. Katy Bernard and Guy Latry (Ventadour, 2012)
TBP	*Guilhem de Peitieus, duc d'Aquitaine, prince du trobar. Trobadas tenues à Bordeaux (Lormont) les 20–21 septembre 2013 et à Poitiers les 12–13 septembre 2014*, ed. Guy Latry and Walter Meliga (Ventadour, 2015)
TD	*Bernard de Ventadour. Folle amour et courtoisie. Trobada tenue à Darnets (près de Centadour) les 9–10 septembre 2015* (Ventadour, 2017)
TH	*Bertran de Born, Seigneur et Troubadour. Trobada tenue à Hautefort les 26 et 27 juin 2009* (Ventadour, 2009)
TR	*Arnaut Daniel, joglar, orfèvre et maístro. Trobada tenue à Ribérac les 29 et 30 juin 2012*, ed. Walter Meliga and Guy Latry (Ventadour, 2013)

Introduction

1 Linda Paterson, *The World of the Troubadours: Medieval Occitan Society, c. 1100–c. 1300* (Cambridge, 1993), pp. 111–14; Giuseppe Noto, *Il giullare e il trovatore nelle liriche e nelle 'biografie' provenzali* (Alessandria, 1998).
2 For Dante, see Chapter Seven; BSC, p. 59.
3 BSC, pp. 39–41.
4 Gérard Gouiran, *L'amour et la guerre. L'oeuvre de Bertran de Born*, 2 vols (Aix-en-Provence, 1985), vol. I, pp. 34, 43–8.
5 See, for example, Guiraut de Borneil's song addressed to Cardalhac, in Ruth V. Sharman, ed., *The Cansos and Sirventes of the Troubadour Giraut de Borneil* (Cambridge, 1989), poem LX.
6 Paterson, *World of the Troubadours*, pp. 1–2.
7 Pierre Bec, *Le comte de Poitiers, premier troubadour. A l'aube d'un verbe et d'une érotique* (Montpellier, 2010), pp. 65–80.
8 Paterson, *World of the Troubadours*, pp. 2–3.
9 *Dizionario*, and the important review by Ruth Harvey in *Tenso*, XXXII (2017), pp. 41–6.
10 = Raimon Escrivan, probably a regular canon (see canons in the table).
11 Ruth Harvey and Linda Paterson, eds, *The Troubadour Tensos and Partimens: A Critical Edition*, 3 vols (Cambridge, 2010), p. 700.
12 Linda Paterson, *Singing the Crusades: French and Occitan Lyric Responses to the Crusading Movements, 1137–1336* (Cambridge, 2018), pp. 239–41.
13 Paterson, *World of the Troubadours*, pp. 225–6.
14 Martin Aurell, '*Fin'amors*, féodalité et *wadd* dans la lyrique des troubadours', in *L'éspace lyrique méditerranéen au Moyen Age: nouvelles approches. Actes du colloque de l'Université de Nantes, 25–7 mars 2004*, ed. Dominique Billy, François Clément and Annie Combes (Toulouse, 2006), pp. 11–15 and 77–88; Paterson, *World of the Troubadours*, pp. 28–36.
15 Paterson, *World of the Troubadours*, p. 153.
16 *Dizionario*, p. 411.
17 Paterson, *World of the Troubadours*, ch. 7, 'Towns'.
18 BSC, p. 491.
19 Saverio Guida, 'Aspetti sociologici delle biografie provenzali', in *Atti del Secondo Congresso della Association Internationale d'Études Occitanes, Torino, 31 agosto–5 settembre 1987*, 2 vols (Turin, 1993), vol. I, pp. 153–63.

20 BSC, pp. 581–2.
21 Ruth Harvey, 'Courtly Culture in Medieval Occitania', in *The Troubadours: An Introduction*, ed. Simon Gaunt and Sarah Kay (Cambridge, 1999), pp. 8–27; Paterson, *World of the Troubadours*, pp. 90–119.
22 Paterson, *World of the Troubadours*, pp. 144–19; Saverio Guida, 'Il quinto bersaglio di Peire d'Alvernhe nella satira *Chantarai d'aquestz trobadors*', *Revista di leteratura medieval*, XXXI (2019), pp. 97–140; Harvey, 'Courtly Culture', p. 12.
23 Paterson, *World of the Troubadours*, pp. 101–3.
24 Ruth Harvey, 'The Professional Status of the Early Troubadours', in *Medieval Occitan Language and Literature: Sixth Annual Conference* (Cambridge, 1991), and Paterson, *World of the Troubadours*, pp. 111–12.
25 See Chapter Eight.
26 Paterson, *Singing*, pp. 192–5.
27 Linda Paterson, 'Les *tensons* et *partimens*', in *Les Troubadours*, ed. Max Rouquette and Tommaso Landolfi, *Europe*, LXXXVI (June–July 2008), pp. 102–14.
28 Pierre Bec, *Burlesque et obscénité chez les troubadours: pour une approche du contre-texte médiéval* (Paris, 1984), and Edmond Faral, *Les jongleurs en France au moyen âge* (Paris, 1971).
29 István Frank, *Répertoire métrique de la poésie des troubadours*, 2 vols (Paris, 1953–7).
30 Dominique Billy, *L'architecture lyrique médiévale. Analyse métrique et modélisation des structures interstrophiques dans la poésie lyrique des troubadours et des trouvères* (Montpellier, 1989).
31 Linda Paterson, *Troubadours and Eloquence* (Oxford, 1975).
32 Francesco Carapezza, 'La dimensione musicale dei trovatori', *Lecturae tropatorum*, XIII (2020), pp. 127–63. For music I am particularly indebted to Carapezza and to Anna Radaelli, who most kindly shared her unpublished work with me.
33 Carapezza, 'La dimensione', pp. 145–6.
34 Ibid., pp. 134–5; Luca Barbieri, 'Le canzoni di crociata e il canone lirico oitanico', *Medioevi*, I (2015), pp. 45–74.
35 BSC, pp. 32, 37, 311.
36 Ibid., p. 63.
37 John Haines, *Medieval Song in Romance Languages* (Cambridge, 2010), pp. 38, 44, 58, 120 and the Appendix on pp. 162–71.
38 Francesco Carapezza, 'Le melodie perdute di Guglielmo IX', in *'Que ben devetz conoisser la plus fina'. Per Margherita Spampinato*,

ed. M. Pagano (Rome, 2018), pp. 177–92; see also Margaret Switten, 'Music and Versification: Fetz Marcabrus los mots e.l so', in *The Troubadours*, ed. Gaunt and Kay, pp. 141–63 (p. 141). For the possible influence of Arabic poetry on William's poetry and in particular his versification, see Martin Aurell, 'Guillaume IX et l'Islam', in *Guilhem de Peitieus, duc d'Aquitaine, prince du trobar*, TBP, pp. 69–126 (especially 119–22, 125).

39 Carapezza, 'Le melodie perdute', p. 180.

40 Switten, 'Music', p. 141.

41 Stefano Asperti, 'Don Johanz la sap: musicisti e lirica romanza in Lombardia nel Trecento', in *Studi di filologia romanza offerti a Valeria Bertolucci Pizzorusso*, ed. Pietro G. Beltrami et al., 2 vols (Pisa, 2006), vol. I, pp. 67–90 (p. 86), cited in Carapezza, 'La dimensione', p. 18.

42 See Chapter One.

43 Carapezza, 'La dimensione', p. 8, and 'Le melodie perdute', pp. 185–6; see also Gerald A. Bond, *The Poetry of William VII, Count of Poitiers, IX Duke of Aquitaine* (New York and London, 1982), pp. 144–5.

44 Carapezza, 'La dimensione', p. 28 and n. 62.

45 Ibid., pp. 28–9.

46 Ibid., pp. 29–30.

47 Ibid., pp. 33–5.

48 John Haines, John Butt and Laurence Dreyfus, *Eight Centuries of Troubadours and Trouvères: The Changing Identity of Medieval Music* (Cambridge, 2004), p. 265.

49 Ibid., p. 283; Margaret Switten, *The Cansos of Raimon de Miraval: A Study of the Poems and Melodies* (Cambridge, MA, 1985), p. 4.

50 Haines et al., *Eight Centuries*, pp. 237–49, 284–92; see also Claudie Chaillou-Amadieu, 'Les exécutions musicales de Guillaume d'Aquitaine: entre réécriture et reconstitution', in TBP, pp. 251–64.

51 Jörn Gruber, *Die Dialektik der Trobar* (Tübingen, 1983).

52 Stefano Milonia, *Rima e melodia nell'arte allusiva dei trovatori* (Rome, 2016), especially pp. 17–18, 24–5, 87–90, 95–6, 102, 147–64.

53 Paterson, *Singing*, p. 15.

54 Paterson, 'Les *tensons*', pp. 108–10.

55 Harvey and Paterson, *Tensos*, pp. 964, 141, 829.

56 Leslie Topsfield, *Troubadours and Love* (Cambridge, 1975), p. 24.

57 Sharman, *The Cansos and Sirventes*, poem XLIX, 23–6.

58 Paterson, *Troubadours and Eloquence*, ch. 4.

59 Paterson, *Singing*, p. 71.
60 Topsfield, *Troubadours and Love*, pp. 14–26.

1 Guilhem IX

1 Jane Martindale, '*Cavalaria et Orgueill*: Duke William IX of Aquitaine and the Historian', in *Status, Authority and Regional Power: Aquitaine and France, 9th to 12th Centuries* (Aldershot, 1997), ch. 10, pp. 91 and 114; Gerald A. Bond, *The Poetry of William VII, Count of Poitiers, IX Duke of Aquitaine* (New York and London, 1982), p. xix; Richard Goddard, *The Early Troubadours and the Latin Tradition*, Universitaire Pers Maastricht (published in 2017 from the original thesis of 1985), especially pp. 35, 40, 43–4, 62.
2 The main edition of reference here is Nicolò Pasero, *Guglielmo IX d'Aquitania, Poesie* (Modena, 1973).
3 Martindale, '*Cavalaria*', pp. 87–116 (pp. 100–104). For an extensive collection of historical documents pertaining to Guilhem, with English translations, see Bond, *Poetry*.
4 Martin Aurell, 'Guillaume IX et l'Islam', in TBP, pp. 69–126 (pp. 77 and 81, n. 58).
5 Bond, *Poetry*, p. xxxiv.
6 Martindale, '*Cavalaria*', p. 103.
7 Goddard, *The Early Troubadours and the Latin Tradition*, p. 33. For other examples, see Aurell, 'Guillaume IX et l'Islam', p. 124.
8 Martindale, '*Cavalaria*', p. 88.
9 Bond, *Poetry*, p. 119.
10 Roger A. B. Mynors, Rodney M. Thomson and Michael Winterbottom, ed. and trans., *Gesta regum Anglorum: The History of the English Kings*, 2 vols (Oxford, 1998), vol. I, pp. 783–4, vol. II, 392, n. 439 (my translation).
11 Aurell, 'Guillaume IX', pp. 107–9; Martindale, '*Cavalaria*', pp. 89–90.
12 Aurell, 'Guillaume IX', p. 83; *Hic audax fuit et probus nimiumque iocundus, facetos etiam histriones facetiis superans multiplicibus* (Orderic Vitalis, *The Ecclesiastical History*, ed. Marjorie Chibnall, 5 vols (Oxford, 1975), vol. X, 20, IV, 118, pp. 324–5; Chibnall's translations have been slightly modified).
13 Orderic Vitalis, vol. X, 21, p. 342; Aurell, 'Guillaume IX', pp. 101–2.
14 Orderic Vitalis, vol. X, p. 343, n. 5; Aurell, 'Guillaume IX', pp. 102 and 107; Michel Banniard, 'Guillaume et le latin de son temps: quelques arrière-plans langagiers', in TBP, pp. 275–86 (pp. 282–3).

15 Banniard, 'Guillaume et le latin de son temps', p. 283.
16 BSC, p. 7.
17 Georges Duby, *The Knight, the Lady and the Priest: The Making of Modern Marriage in Medieval France* (Harmondsworth, 1985), pp. 4–10; Aurell, 'Guillaume IX', p. 89; Linda Paterson, *The World of the Troubadours: Medieval Occitan Society, c. 1100–c. 1300* (Cambridge, 1993), pp. 228, 312–16 and 338.
18 Ruth Harvey, 'The Wives of the "First Troubadour", Duke William IX of Aquitaine', *Journal of Medieval History*, XIX (1993), pp. 307–25 (pp. 324 and 315).
19 Goddard, *Early Troubadours*, pp. 32–3 and 62; Martindale, '*Cavalaria*', pp. 99 and 116.
20 Francesco Carapezza, 'La dimensione musicale dei trovatori', LT, XIII (2020), p. 180.
21 Bond, *Poetry*, p. 59, n. 25; for more about Eble see Chapter Four.
22 Linda Paterson, *Troubadours and Eloquence* (Oxford, 1975), pp. 26–8.
23 Guglielmo di Poitiers, 'Molt jauzens mi prenc an amar' (BdT 183.8), in LT, ed. Costanzo di Girolamo, VII (2014).
24 Linda Paterson, '*Fin'amor* and the Development of the Courtly *Canso*', in *The Troubadours: An Introduction*, ed. Simon Gaunt and Sarah Kay (Cambridge, 1999), pp. 28–31 (pp. 30–31); Alexander J. Denomy, '*Fin'amors*: The Pure Love of the Troubadours, Its Amorality and Possible Source', *Medieval Studies*, VII (1945), pp. 139–207 (p. 144).
25 For fuller discussion see Paterson, '*Fin'amor*'.
26 Alessandro Bampa, 'La maturité du corpus du "premier troubadour"', TBP, pp. 205–17, argues that from both formal and content perspectives 'le corpus de Guillaume est très abouti [highly developed]', and see Walter Meliga, 'La postérité du comte de Poitiers', ibid., pp. 343–52.
27 His fear and provision for his young son exclude the idea that it was composed just before the duke's death in 1126, when his son would have been in his late twenties. In reference to Aurell, 'Guillaume IX', pp. 87–9, I share Meliga's view that Guilhem was not about to leave on his 1101 crusade: it would be strange to contemplate a crusade with the idea of death as a foregone conclusion, rather than with the intention to serve God's cause.
28 Silvio Melani, 'Il cammino della croce e gli artigli della lussuria: ipotesi sulle "perdute" *cantilenae* composte da Guglielmo IX in occasione della sua crociata', in *Le letterature romanze del Medioevo:*

testi, storia, intersezioni. Atti del v *Convegno Nazionale della* SIFR, ed. Antonio Pioletti (Rome, 2000), pp. 281–93 (p. 285).

29 Paterson, *World of the Troubadours*, ch. 4.

2 Jaufre Rudel

1 See Giorgio Chiarini, *Il canzoniere di Jaufre Rudel* (L'Aquila, 1985), p. 53.

2 'Hear how this song progresses and improves and Marcabru, according to his pure intentions (*or* flawless judgment), knows how to make and bind up the theme of the *vers* so that no-one can erase a word from it.' Simon Gaunt, Ruth Harvey and Linda Paterson, *Marcabru: A Critical Edition* (Cambridge, 2000), poem IX, pp. 1–4.

3 For the historical background see Sébastien-Abel Laurent, 'Le troubadour Jaufre Rudel de Blaye: un proche des ducs d'Aquitaine devenu rebelle?', in *Fidélités et dissidences. Actes du* XII*e congrès de l'Association internationale des Études occitanes, Albi, 10–15 juillet 2017*, ed. Jean-François Courouau and David Fabié (Toulouse, 2020), pp. 499–508; Frédéric Boutoulle, 'L'appel du large. Jaufre Rudel et les autres seigneurs de Blaye aux XIe, XIIe et XIIIe siècles', in TB, pp. 81–101 (especially pp. 82–3 and 101); Walter Meliga, 'Brève récapitulation de l'amor de lonh', in TB, pp. 172–85 (pp. 174–5). In the same volume Robert Lug ('Jaufre Rudel rajeuni', pp. 57–79) attempted to redate Jaufre to the early thirteenth century, though this was not accepted by others there: apart from Meliga and Boutoulle, see Roy Rosenstein, 'Jaufre Rudel au pluriel: les Jaufre Rudel de Blaya et d'ailleurs', in TB, pp. 103–14 (p. 104).

4 The edition of reference is Chiarini, *Jaufre Rudel*, apart from poem IV; for Hugh VII of Lusignan see p. 19 of the edition.

5 Rosenstein, 'Jaufre Rudel au pluriel', p. 110.

6 See Meliga, 'Brève récapitulation', p. 175.

7 Translation of Chiarini's edition, p. 52.

8 Pierre Bec, 'Jaufre Rudel et les poètes romantiques allemands', TB, pp. 21–34 (p. 22).

9 François Zufferey, 'Nouvelle approche de l'amour de loin', *Cultura Neolatina*, LXIX (2009), pp. 7–58.

10 For *bels digz* Chiarini prints *cortes ginh*, 'cortesa sagacia', from mss. CM – perhaps better 'courtly art'.

11 Zufferey, 'Nouvelle approche', p. 39, 'est pour moi un tel obstacle'; for 'deferred' see DOM s.v. *aïs*.

12 For a summary of approaches see Meliga, 'Brève récapitulation'.

13 For a different interpretation of *chaitius* see Lucia Lazzerini, 'Chaitius clamatz clé d'une chanson de croisade?', in TB, pp. 186–96, especially p. 191.
14 Stanley Stewart, *The Enclosed Garden: The Tradition and the Image in Seventeenth-Century Poetry* (Madison, WI, 1966), especially pp. 15–16, 19, 31, 35, 43.
15 For a mystical interpretation see Lucia Lazzerini, *Les troubadours et la sagesse* (Ventadour, 2013), ch. 3.
16 Several manuscripts replace the better-reading *portz* with the more general *pas*: see Zufferey, 'Nouvelle approche', p. 48. For *portz* in journeys to the Holy Land see Joseph Linskill, *The Poems of the Troubadour Raimbaut de Vaqueiras* (The Hague, 1964), poem XXII, 83–4, who writes of opening up *los camins e.ls portz/ de Brandiz tro als Bratz Sain Jorz*.
17 Zufferey, 'Nouvelle approche', p. 54.
18 Peter Dronke, 'The Song of Songs and Medieval Love-Lyric', in *The Bible and Medieval Culture*, ed. Willem Lourdaux and Daniël Verhelst (Leuven, 1979), pp. 237–62 (pp. 259–60), cited in E. Ann Matter, *The Voice of My Beloved: The Song of Songs in Western Medieval Christianity* (Philadelphia, PA, 2010), p. 191.
19 Laurent, 'Le troubadour Jaufre Rudel', pp. 499–508 (p. 505).
20 For songs of separation see Linda Paterson, *Singing the Crusades: French and Occitan Lyric Responses to the Crusading Movements, 1137–1336* (Cambridge, 2018), p. 321 (Index), *chansons de départie*.
21 Gaunt, Harvey and Paterson, *Marcabru*, poem VII, 1–7.
22 Di Girolamo, *I trovatori* (Turin, 1989), p. 88, thought that because Marcabru sent a song to Jaufre Rudel in the Holy Land he must have had some liking for him; however, Marcabru couples his dedication to Jaufre with a comment about the French, which is probably a sly jibe at their queen's alleged scandalous behaviour there (see Gaunt, Harvey and Paterson, *Marcabru*, p. 207, n. 9).
23 Rosenstein, 'Jaufre Rudel au pluriel', p. 113, and Lazzerini, 'Chaitius clamatz', p. 196.

3 Marcabru

1 Simon Gaunt, Ruth Harvey and Linda Paterson, *Marcabru: A Critical Edition* (Cambridge, 2000), henceforth *Marcabru*, is the edition of reference. All texts are accessible on Rialto: www.rialto.unina.it.
2 *Marcabru*, p. 1 and n. 2.

3 For a detailed critique see Ruth Harvey, 'The Troubadour Marcabru and His Public', *Reading Medieval Studies*, XIV (1988), pp. 47–76, especially p. 56.
4 *Marcabru*, poems XLIII and XX.
5 Ruth Harvey, *The Troubadour Marcabru and Love* (London, 1989), pp. 13–17.
6 Harvey, 'The Troubadour Marcabru and His Public', especially p. 57.
7 Ibid., p. 51.
8 *Marcabru*, p. 3.
9 For the dating and chronology of Marcabru's compositions see *Marcabru*, pp. 2–5, and the 'Dating' sections of individual texts.
10 *Marcabru*, p. 4; Linda Paterson, *Singing the Crusades: French and Occitan Lyric Responses to the Crusading Movements, 1137–1336* (Cambridge, 2018), pp. 34–8.
11 Paterson, *Singing*, p. 34.
12 Valeria Tortoreto, ed., *Il trovatore Cercamon* (Modena, 1981), poem VI, 43–8.
13 See, for example, Alcuin Blamires with Karen Pratt and C. William Marx, ed., *Woman Defamed and Woman Defended: An Anthology of Medieval Texts* (Oxford, 1992).
14 Anthony Weir and James Jerman, *Images of Lust: Sexual Carvings on Medieval Churches* (London, 1986).
15 Linda Paterson, *Troubadours and Eloquence* (Oxford, 1975), pp. 28–9.
16 Angelica Rieger, *Trobairitz. Der Beitrag der Frau in der altokzitanischen höfischen Lyrik* (Tübingen, 1991), pp. 45, 25–30.
17 See, for example, James A. Brundage, *Law, Sex, and Christian Society in Medieval Europe* (Chicago, IL, 1987), pp. 234–5.
18 *Marcabru*, p. 5 and n. 19.
19 Vincent Pollina, 'Les mélodies du troubadour Marcabru: questions de style et de genre', in *Atti del Secondo Congresso Internazionale delle 'Association Internationale d'Études Occitanes'*, ed. Giuliano Gasca Queirazza, 2 vols (Turin, 1993), vol. I, pp. 289–306 (pp. 299–300); *Marcabru*, p. 26. For an edition of the melodies see Samuel Rosenberg, Margaret Switten and Gérard Le Vot, *Songs of the Troubadours and Trouvères: An Anthology of Poems and Melodies* (New York and London, 1998), pp. 47–51.
20 See Introduction.
21 *Marcabru*, p. 410, n. 2; Francesco Carapezza, 'La dimensione musicale dei trovatori', LT, XIII (2020), pp. 127–63, p. 35.
22 *Marcabru*, pp. 13–18.

23 *Marcabru*, pp. 20–26, and p. 190 where the structure of XIV is set out schematically.
24 Paterson, *Troubadours and Eloquence*, ch. 1.
25 Harvey, 'The Troubadour Marcabru and His Public', especially pp. 61–6.
26 Aniello Fratta, *Peire d'Alvernhe, Poesie* (Rome, 1996), pp. 4, 22–8 and 38–42. For the meaning of *que fai avol demostransa* ('who shows baseness') see Paterson, *Troubadours and Eloquence*, p. 14, n. 6.

4 Bernart de Ventadorn

1 Moshé Lazar, *Bernard de Ventadour, troubadour du XIIe siècle: chansons d'amour* (Paris, 1966), p. 9; see also Martín de Riquer, *Los Trovadores*, 3 vols (Barcelona, 1975), vol. I, p. 346. The edition of reference is that of Stephen G. Nichols, *The Songs of Bernart de Ventadorn* (Chapel Hill, NC, 1962).
2 Lazar, *Bernard*, pp. 45–8.
3 BSC, pp. 20–28 and songs 26, 36–48 and 33, 43–5.
4 Saverio Guida, 'Il quinto bersaglio di Peire d'Alvernhe nella satira *Chantarai d'aquestz trobadors*', *Revista di leteratura medieval*, XXXI (2019), pp. 97–140; see also Linda Paterson, 'Centres et périphéries: la civilisation littéraire occitane et son espacement dans le temps et les régions', p. 88, in press.
5 323.11, 19–24, Riquer, *Trovadores*, vol. I, p. 335. The rhyme-words of this stanza of the satire are based on Bernart's *Be m'an perdut lai enves Ventadorn* (12, 8–14), where Bernart says he rushed towards love like a fish to the bait and before he knew it he was in the midst of the flames burning him more than the fire in an oven. Ideas of stoking the castle bread-oven, whether on the part of his 'father' or 'mother', may play on common troubadour images of bread and fire as sex.
6 Riquer, *Trovadores*, vol. I, p. 344 and n. 11.
7 Pierre Bec, *Le comte de Poitiers, premier troubadour. A l'aube d'un verbe et d'une érotique* (Montpellier, 2010), p. 25. The word *gratiosus* does not mean 'charming' (Bec 'grâce au charme de ses chansons') or 'gracioso' (Riquer, *Trovadores*, vol. I, p. 142).
8 Valeria Tortoreto, ed., *Il trovatore Cercamon* (Modena, 1981), poem VII; 63.8, ed. Fabrizio Beggiato, *Il trovatore Bernart Marti* (Modena, 1984), poem VII, 57–60.
9 LR, III, 442a 'jouissance, possession'; see also Ruth V. Sharman, *The Cansos and Sirventes of the Troubadour Giraut de Borneil* (Cambridge,

1989), poem x, 7–8, *Qe.m ditz que gauzida/ N'aurai ses faillia*, 'which promises me assured enjoyment from her'.

10 *Marcabru*, poem xxxi, 73–9, 37–8, 21–2, 39–40.

11 This reading emerges from only one of the eight manuscripts, but see the editors' note to v. 79 on p. 400.

12 Richard Goddard, *The Early Troubadours and the Latin Tradition* (Maastricht, 2017), pp. 54–5. It is unclear why William should praise Eble's industry, unless it is a humorous reference to the work he had to go to in preparing the dinner.

13 Linda Paterson, '*Fin'amor* and the Development of the Courtly *Canso*', in *The Troubadours: An Introduction*, ed. Simon Gaunt and Sarah Kay (Cambridge, 1999), pp. 3–33.

14 Marcabru's period of activity can be dated to as late as 1149, perhaps even 1154. See *Marcabru*, p. 2, which postdates the viscount's death in 1147.

15 See Paterson, 'The Development', pp. 33–5.

16 Questions of how far *fin'amor* is adulterous or heretical have been much debated. For a brief summary see Paterson, 'The Development', pp. 35–8.

17 This and other songs of Bernart are beautifully sung on the Ensemble Beatus's *Trobar: Chansons d'amour, de la Vierge à la Dame* (www.libraria-occitana.org).

18 Frederick Goldin, *The Mirror of Narcissus in the Courtly Love Lyric* (Ithaca, NY 1968), p. 98 ('As he believed the lady was a mirror of perfection, so he believed that in casting his own image in that mirror he would be united with the ideal, the light of the world, the living form of Beauty'); L. Lazzerini, 'Le chant de Bernart de Ventadorn entre motifs folkloriques et postérité poético-théologique', in TD, pp. 45–63.

19 Sarah Kay, 'Love in a Mirror: An Aspect of the Imagery of Bernart de Ventadorn', *Medium Aevum*, LII (1983), pp. 272–85.

20 Ibid., pp. 277–8.

21 Ibid., p. 278.

22 The order of stanzas in a composition such as this, where all follow the same versification and rhyme scheme, is notoriously unstable in transmission.

23 Kay, 'Love in a Mirror', p. 280. For the tricky notion of 'feudalism' in an Occitan context see Linda Paterson, *The World of the Troubadours: Medieval Occitan Society, c. 1100–c. 1300* (Cambridge, 1993), ch. 2.

24 Nichols (*The Songs*, p. 17) explores the 'subtle and varied form which he made of the stanza', the 'subtlety and finesse' of his

rhymes, and his development of the use of feminine rhymes, attributing 'the tonal richness of his poems to the fact that only twelve of the forty-one are without any feminine rhyme'.

25 István Frank, *Répertoire métrique de la poésie des troubadours*, 2 vols (Paris, 1953–7), vol. 1, p. 44. For a fuller visualization see the editions of Nichols, *The Songs*, p. 20 or Lazar, *Bernard de Ventadour*, p. 32. Lazar sets out in detail the simple and complex combinations of Bernart's rhymes on pp. 33–6.

26 Anna Ferrari, 'Bernart de Ventadorn ou l'apogée de la courtoisie', TD, pp. 77–92 (pp. 85–7).

27 Nichols, *The Songs*, pp. 22–3, and see above.

28 Francesco Carapezza, 'Ecouter Bernart de Ventadorn. Lecture de quatre *unica* musicaux: BdT 70.42 (X), 24 (W), 17 (G) et 25 (R)', in TD, pp. 3–12.

29 Ferrari, 'Bernart de Ventadorn', p. 81, writes of his creation of a 'brand'.

5 The *Trobairitz*

1 François Zufferey, 'Toward a Delimitation of the Trobairitz Corpus', in *The Voice of the Trobairitz: Perspectives on the Women Troubadours*, ed. William D. Paden (Philadelphia, PA, 1989), pp. 31–43. See also Maria V. Rodriguez Winiarski's overview, 'The *Trobairitz*', www.trob-eu.net, accessed 7 July 2023.

2 The edition of reference unless otherwise stated is Angelica Rieger, *Trobairitz. Der Beitrag der Frau in der altokzitanischen höfischen Lyrik* (Tübingen, 1991). Women writing in French include Marie de France, Clemence of Barking and Marguerite Porete; for women writing in Latin see Peter Dronke, *Women Writers of the Middle Ages: A Critical Study of Texts from Perpetua (d. 203) to Marguerite Porete (d. 1310)* (Cambridge, 1984), especially pp. 84–106. The best English anthology of editions with translations, with an excellent introduction, is *Songs of the Women Troubadours* by Matilda Bruckner, Laurie Shepard and Sarah White (New York and London, 1995); see also Pierre Bec's important *Chants d'amour des femmes troubadours* (Paris, 1995).

3 BSC, p. 380, §§ 10–11; see also Rieger, *Trobairitz*, pp. 93–153.

4 Linda Paterson, *The World of the Troubadours: Medieval Occitan Society, c. 1100–c. 1300* (Cambridge, 1993), pp. 220–28.

5 The one *canso* attributed to Bieiris de Romans and addressed to *Na Maria* is sometimes thought to be a song of lesbian love (see

Bruckner, Shepard and White, *Songs*, p. 153). However, the name could well be a mangling of *N'Albric de Roman* (*Dizionario*, p. 126), and the song therefore be male authored.

6 René Nelli, *L'Erotique des troubadours* (Toulouse, 1963), pp. 199–209.

7 Martín de Riquer, ed., *Los Trovadores*, 3 vols (Barcelona, 1975), vol. I, p. 462, poem 79, 33–40.

8 Ibid., vol. II, pp. 794–5, poem 153, 9–24.

9 Bruckner, Shepard and White, *Songs*, p. xxv. For examples see ibid., pp. 130–37, and Bec, *Chants d'amour*, pp. 195–231.

10 BdT 461.201, stanzas I, II and IV, in Bec, *Chants d'amour*, p. 222.

11 Angelica Rieger, '"Ins e.l cor port, dona, vostre faisso". Image et imaginaire de la femme à travers l'enluminure dans les chansonniers des troubadours', *Cahiers de Civilisation Médiévale*, XXVII (1985), pp. 385–415.

12 *Dizionario*, p. 77, and Riquer, *Trovadores*, vol. I, pp. 79, 17–24.

13 See Walter T. Pattison, *The Life and Works of the Troubadour Raimbaut d'Orange* (Minneapolis, MN, 1952), poem XV. Azalais echoes his rhyme-word *fanc* in her *faigna*, and the rhyme-sound *-ais* found in the last three lines of each of his stanzas.

14 See Paterson, *World of the Troubadours*, p. 262, and the references in n. 136, and particularly Sarah Kay, *Subjectivity in Troubadour Poetry* (Cambridge, 1990), pp. 103–4.

15 Sarah Kay, 'Derivation, Derived Rhyme, and the Trobairitz', in *Voice*, ed. Paden, pp. 157–82.

16 See Ismael Fernández de la Cuesta and Robert Lafont, *Las Cançons dels trobadors* (Toulouse, 1979), p. 316. Several performances are on YouTube.

17 Riquer, *Los Trovadores*, vol. II, poem 156, 4–8, 29–30.

18 Bruckner, Shephard and White, *Songs*, p. xxxi.

19 Riquer, *Los Trovadores*, vol. II, poem 153, 1–8.

20 Kay, 'Derivation', p. 167.

21 Ibid., p. 168.

22 Linda Paterson, *Singing the Crusades: French and Occitan Lyric Responses to the Crusading Movements, 1137–1336* (Cambridge, 2018), p. 17.

23 See www.rialto.unina.it, accessed 7 July 2023.

24 Rieger, *Trobairitz*, p. 725; Paterson, *Singing*, pp. 161–2. For the text see www.rialto.unina.it, accessed 7 July 2023.

25 Paolo Di Luca, '*Sirventesca*: le sirventes parodié', *Revue des langues romanes*, CXII (2008), pp. 405–34, especially pp. 417–26.

26 Stefano Asperti, *Il trovatore Raimon Jordan* (Modena, 1990), pp. 118–19.

27 See, for example, Alcuin Blamires with Karen Pratt and C. William Marx, eds, *Woman Defamed and Woman Defended: An Anthology of Medieval Texts* (Oxford, 1992).
28 Giuseppe E. Sansone, *Testi didattico-cortese di Provenza* (Bari, 1977), p. 243, vv. 230–33.
29 For her life and political role see Thierry Pécout, *L'invention de la Provence: Raymond Bérenger v* (Paris, 2004), pp. 112–14, and index under Gersende de Forcalquier and Gersende de Sabran.
30 BSC, p. 215.
31 Paolo Di Luca, ed., 'Blacasset, *Se·l mals d'amor m'auzi ni m'es noisens* (BdT 96.10a), Pujol, *Dieus es amors e verais salvamens* (BdT 386.2), Alaisina ~ Carenza, *Na Carenza al bel cors avenenç* (BdT 12.1 = 108.1)', in LT, IV (2011), which supersedes my earlier edition on Rialto.
32 See DOM s.v. *carencia* and the references.
33 Rieger, *Trobairitz*, pp. 262–74; BSC, pp. 202–3.
34 Ruth Harvey and Linda Paterson, ed., *The Troubadour Tensos and Partimens: A Critical Edition*, 3 vols (Cambridge, 2010), vol. III, p. 934.
35 See ibid., vol. I, pp. xxxii–xxxix.
36 Ibid., vol. III, pp. 902–12.
37 Ibid., vol. II, pp. 841–9.
38 Linda Paterson, 'Greeks and Latins at the Time of the Fourth Crusade: Patriarch John x Kamateros and a Troubadour *Tenso*', in *Languages of Love and Hate: Conflict, Communication, and Identity in the Medieval Mediterranean*, ed. Sarah Lambert and Helen Nicholson (Turnhout, 2012), pp. 119–39.
39 Giosué Lachin, ed., *Il trovatore Elias Cairel* (Modena, 2004), poem II, 54–60.
40 Paterson, 'Greeks and Latins', pp. 128–37, though see Luciano Formisano, 'Prospettive di ricerca sui canzonieri d'autore nella lira d'oïl', in *La filologia romanza e i codici. Atti del convegno, Messina, Università degli studi, Facoltà di lettere e filosofia, 19–22 decembre 1991*, ed. Saverio Guida and Fortunata Latella, 2 vols (Messina, 1994), vol. I, pp. 131–52 (p. 145).

6 Arnaut Daniel

1 Robert M. Durling, ed. and trans., *The Divine Comedy of Dante Alighieri*, 3 vols (Oxford, 2003), vol. II: *Purgatorio*, Canto XXVI, 140–47.

2 The edition of reference is Gianluigi Toja, *Arnaut Daniel: Canzoni* (Florence, 1960), with the exception of songs VIII, which is set out as in Martín de Riquer's *Los Trovadores* (Barcelona, 1975), pp. 624–7, and XVIII, where the edition is that of Mario Eusebi, *Arnaut Daniel: 'L'aur'amara* (Milan, 1984).

3 Dante, *De Vulgari Eloquentia*, ed. Steven Botterill (Cambridge, 2009), II, ii, 8; II, vi, 6; II, xiii, 2.

4 See Walter Meliga, 'Conclusion de la *Trobada*', in TR, pp. 145–51 (pp. 150–51), citing Francesco Petrarca, *Trionfi, rime estravaganti, codice degli abbozzi*, ed. Vinicio Pacca and Laura Paolino (Milan, 1996), poem IV, vv. 40–41.

5 See Peter Makin, *Provence and Pound* (Berkeley, CA, and London, 1978), and Jacques Roubaud, *Les Troubadours. Anthologie bilingue* (Paris, 1980).

6 Compare Riquer, *Trovadores*, p. 605, and Pierre Bec, *Arnaut Daniel. 'Fin' amor' et folie du verbe* (Paris, 2012), p. 10, who propose dates of 1180–95, with Maurizio Perugi, 'Arnaut Daniel, un troubadour de renommée internationale', in TR, pp. 29–38 (p. 33) (1174–6 and 1190–91).

7 *Non puosc mudar mon chantar non esparga*, ed. Gérard Gouiran, *L'amour et la guerre: L'oeuvre de Bertran de Born*, 2 vols (Aix-en-Provence, 1985). Poem 28 is modelled on Arnaut's *Si.m fos Amors de ioi donar tant larga*, ed. Toja, *Arnaut Daniel*, song XVII.

8 BSC, p. 59; *Dizionario*, p. 59.

9 Helen Waddell, *The Wandering Scholars* (London and Toronto, 1927, repr. 1942) and *Medieval Latin Lyrics* (Harmondsworth, 1929, repr. 1962). For Raimon de Durfort see Toja, *Arnaut Daniel*, p. 190, vv. 29–32 and 37, and for a modern French translation of the exchange see Pierre Bec, *Burlesque et obscénité chez les troubadours: pour une approche du contre-texte médiéval* (Paris, 1984), pp. 140–53.

10 René Lavaud and René Nelli, *Les troubadours. Jaufre, Flamenca, Barlaam et Josaphat* (Paris, 1969), vv. 1706–10.

11 Gouiran, *L'amour et la guerre*, pp. 38, 42; Francesco Carapezza, 'Le côté musical d'Arnaut Daniel: remarques sur les structures strophiques de ses chansons', in TR, pp. 55–75 (p. 57).

12 Dominique Pauvert, with Christine Escarmant, 'Arnaut Daniel, maître du *cornar ric*', TR, pp. 39–53 (pp. 39–40).

13 See fr.wikipedia.org, accessed 7 July 2023.

14 Martín de Riquer, ed., *Los Trovadores* (Barcelona, 1975), vol. II, poem 207, 43–8.

15 Ibid., poem x, 43–6.
16 Dominique Billy, 'L'art poétique d'Arnaut Daniel', in TR, pp. 107–31 (p. 126 and n. 51).
17 See Linda Paterson, *Troubadours and Eloquence* (Oxford, 1975), pp. 187–90.
18 Toja, *Arnaut Daniel*, p. 254 but set out with internal rhymes as by Riquer in his *Trovadores*, vol. II, p. 624; Toja presents a new line after each rhyme.
19 Paterson, *Troubadours and Eloquence*, pp. 86–7 and 204.
20 Roy Rosenstein, 'Arnaut Daniel parle-t-il portugais?', and Jacques Roubaud, 'L'Etrange destin de la *canson* "Lo ferm voler" d'Arnaut Daniel', in TR, pp. 93–106 and 133–43.
21 The complexity of this song has led to differences in the establishment of the text from the 22 manuscript versions, and in the interpretation of some of its details, though the only really important divergences concern the *tornada*. The edition here is Eusebi's *Arnaut Daniel* (p. 157) with the modification in the *tornada* proposed by Fratta: see www.rialto.unina.it, accessed 7 July 2023.
22 My thanks go to Mike Paterson for his analysis, explanations and diagrams.
23 For other discussions of the song's structure see Dominique Billy, *L'architecture lyrique médiévale. Analyse métrique et modélisation des structures interstrophiques dans la poésie lyrique des troubadours et des trouvères* (Montpellier, 1989), pp. 198–202, his 'L'art poétique', pp. 122–4, and Roubaud, 'L'Etrange destin'.
24 For this conceit compare Linda Paterson, 'Anonymous (Nompar de Caumont?), *Finament* (BdT 461.122)', in LT (2014), stanza x.
25 Carapezza regards the interpretation of *son* as 'melody' as extremely doubtful ('Le côté musical d'Arnaut Daniel: remarques sur les structures strophiques de ses chansons', in TR, pp. 67–8).
26 Carapezza, 'Le côté musical', pp. 60–61, 69 for a modern transcription, and 75.

7 Bertran de Born

1 Much has been added by the book by Jean-Pierre Thuillat, *Bertran de Born. Histoire et légende* (Périgueux, 2009), on which this chapter heavily draws. The text of reference here is that of Gérard Gouiran, *L'amour et la guerre. L'oeuvre de Bertran de Born*, 2 vols (Aix-en-Provence, 1985). That of William D. Paden, Tilda Sankovitch and

Patricia H. Stäblein, *The Poems of the Troubadour Bertran de Born* (Berkeley, CA, and London, 1986; henceforth PSS) contains much useful historical information, and their poem numbering is added in brackets after the Gouiran references. I am deeply grateful to Ruth Harvey for help with the complexities of the historical background.

2 Thuillat, *Betran de Born*, pp. 19–21 and 23.
3 Ibid., pp. 67–73, 86, 90–95, 97–100.
4 Gouiran, *L'amour*, p. 175.
5 Ibid., p. 176.
6 Thuillat, *Betran de Born*, pp. 109–11.
7 Ibid., pp. 116–20.
8 PSS, p. 176.
9 10, 1–24 (PSS 10).
10 None of the attempted explanations of 'Sir Carter' is particularly convincing: see Gouiran's edition, p. 196, and the summary in PSS, p. 181, n.13. The simplest explanation may be that Henry is a 'Sir' by birth but a peasant by poverty.
11 For the translation of *malvatz* in v. 8, which Gouiran translates as 'médiocres', see his note on p. 214: 'Je pense que ce mot souligne la médiocrité de ceux qu'il caractérise, mais cette notion ne doit pas être séparée de la lâcheté.'
12 Thuillat, *Betran de Born*, p. 161; 11, 2–10 and 25–32 (PSS 11).
13 Ibid., p. 166.
14 12, 1–6 (PSS 14); 13 (PSS 15); Gouiran, *L'amour*, pp. 177–80; Thuillat, *Betran de Born*, pp. 183–4, 211.
15 Thuillat, *Betran de Born*, pp. 215–17, for a plausible scenario.
16 16, 8 (PSS 3), cf. 18, 3 (PSS 19), and Walter Meliga, 'Le *sen* de Bertran de Born', in TH, pp. 21–32.
17 9.3 (PSS 1); 29, 3 and 43 (PSS 33).
18 23 (PSS 21) and 24 (PSS 22).
19 Stefano Asperti, 'L'eredità lirica di Bertran de Born', *Cultura Neolatina*, LXIV (2004), pp. 475–525 (p. 478); BSC, p. 68; Francesco Carapezza, 'Canzoni "date in moglie" a sirventesi nella *vida II* di Bertran de Born', *Cultura Neolatina*, LXVIII (2008), pp. 315–33; 11, 25 (PSS 11), modelled on BdT 242.69.
20 DVE, II, ii. 7–8; *Divine Comedy*, I, XXVIII, 119–22, 134–41; see also Stefano Asperti, 'Miei-sirventes vueilh far dels reis amdos (BdT 80,25)', *Cultura Neolatina*, LVIII (1998), pp. 165–323 (p. 316), who casts doubt on the authorship of *inter alia* 32 (PSS 38), 37 (PSS 30), 45 (PSS 47), 47 (PSS 28).
21 9, 45–6 (PSS 1).

22 26, 29–35, 50–53 (PSS 32).
23 29, 1–7, 36–42 (PSS 33).
24 31, 51–60 (PSS 37).
25 30, 25–32 (PSS 42).
26 35, 1–16 (PSS 44).
27 15, 23–6 (PSS 2).
28 13, 5–24, 19–23, 29–37 (PSS 15); cf. 28, 2–8 (PSS 34) and 36,1–8, 17–23 (PSS 43).
29 Asperti, 'Miei-sirventes', pp. 317–18.
30 See Gouiran, *L'amour*, pp. xxxii–xxxiii.
31 28, 9–14 (PSS 34).
32 8, 78–82 (PSS 20); 6, 31 (PSS 20) and cf 5, 32 (PSS 5) and 38, 10 (PSS 30).
33 For their relationship see Gouiran, *L'amour*, pp. xlii–xliv and lxxii–lxxiii, and Luca Barbieri, 'A *mon Ynsombart part Troia*. Une polémique anti-courtoise dans le dialoque entre trouvères et troubadours', *Medioevo Romanzo*, XXXVII (2013), pp. 264–95.
34 33, 1–12 (PSS 36).
35 34, 1–7 (PSS 41). The text appears to have been reworked at least twice: see Linda Paterson, *Singing the Crusades: French and Occitan Lyric Responses to the Crusading Movements, 1137–1336* (Cambridge, 2018), pp. 78–9.
36 34, 8–14 (PSS 41), M version.
37 Thuillat, *Betran de Born*, p. 240; Paterson, *Singing*, p. 36 and n. 20.
38 Gérard Gouiran, 'Bertran de Born, poète de l'amour', in *Chrétien de Troyes and the Troubadours: Essays in Memory of the late L. Topsfield*, ed. Peter Noble and Linda Paterson (Cambridge, 1984), pp. 52–6; see also his edition, p. xci.
39 17, 76–9 (PSS 17); 3, 25–36 (PSS 8).
40 Thuillat, *Betran de Born*, p. 166, citing John Gillingham, *Richard Coeur de Lion* (Paris, 1996), p. 134.
41 Ibid., p. 176; 2, 28 (PSS 9); cf. 27, 34–5 (PSS 35), where he presents Richard himself joking together about Philip.
42 3, 49–60 (PSS 8).
43 For example, 29, 46–8 (PSS 33).
44 26, 1–21 (PSS 32), and see Gouiran's notes.
45 21, 1–8 (PSS 23).
46 See Chapter Four.
47 9, 1–6 (PSS 1), dating insecure.
48 17, 48–9 (PSS 17); 28, 14–15 (PSS 34); 27, 34–5 (PSS 35); 34, ms. M, 15–21, Gouiran, *L'amour*, p. 684.

49 12, 43–5 (PSS 14); 28, 43–4 (PSS 34).
50 43, 1–9 (PSS 45); Thuillat, *Betran de Born*, p. 265.

8 Raimbaut de Vaqueiras

1 Federico Saviotti, 'Il viaggio del poeta e il viaggio del testo: per un approccio geografico a Raimbaut de Vaqueiras e alla sua tradizione manoscritta', *Moderna*, x (2008), Fascicle 2, pp. 43–59. See also Gilda Caïti-Russo, *Les troubadours à la cour des Malaspina* (Montpellier, 2005).
2 Epic Letter, I, 1–10. References are to Joseph Linskill, *The Poems of the Troubadour Raimbaut de Vaqueiras* (The Hague, 1964).
3 Epic Letter, I, 11–35, I, 39–43, II, 59–62.
4 After the conquest of Constantinople there was an election to decide who should rule the new Latin empire. Boniface lost to Baldwin, and a rift developed between them over Boniface's claim to the throne of Thessalonica. See Linda Paterson, *Singing the Crusades: French and Occitan Lyric Responses to the Crusading Movements, 1137–1336* (Cambridge, 2018), p. 112.
5 See Linda Paterson, *The World of the Troubadours: Medieval Occitan Society, c. 1100–c. 1300* (Cambridge, 1993), ch. 4, 'The Knight and Chivalry'.
6 Ibid., p. 62, and the references to Jean Flori in n. 2.
7 IX, 47–8. For squires see Paterson, *World of the Troubadours*, pp. 82–4.
8 The *razo* in the later ms P, however, relates a dream-like scene in which Raimbaut secretly watches his lady Bel Cavalier, alone, dub herself knight with her brother Boniface's sword.
9 Epic Letter, II, 34–5.
10 VIII, 16.
11 V, 25–6.
12 V, VI, VII, VIII, and see Linskill, *Raimbaut*, p. 16.
13 VII, 1–9; VIII, 9–15. The *descort* was a poem of irregular or variable stanzaic form; Linkskill's translation 'discords' attempts to convey this as well as the idea of quarrelling. See poem XVII.
14 V, 37–9, VI, 21–2.
15 Poems X, XI.
16 XII, 1–8; cf. XIII, 1–8.
17 XVII, 51–2. For a psychological interpretation of this *senhal* in the light of the *razo* in ms P, see William E. Burgwinkle, 'Raimbaut de

Vaqueiras et les rites de l'identité', in *Scène, évolution, sort de la langue et de la littérature d'oc. Actes du Septième Congrès International d'Études Occitanes, Reggio Calabria–Messina, 7–13 juillet 2002*, ed. Rossana Castano, Saverio Guida and Fortunata Latella, 2 vols (Rome, 2003), vol. I, pp. 157–65; see also F. Saviotti, '*Senhals* et pseudonymes, entre Raimon de Cornet et Raimbaut de Vaqueiras', in *Actes du XXVIIe Congrès international de linguistique et de philologie romanes (Nancy, 15–20 juillet 2013). Section 14: Littératures médiévales, Nancy*, ed. Isabel de Riquer, Dominique Billy and Giovanni Palumbo (Nancy, 2017), pp. 195–204, who suggests that Bel Cavalier might be an alter ego for Raimbaut himself.

18 Ruth Harvey and Linda Paterson, eds, *The Troubadour Tensos and Partimens: A Critical Edition*, 3 vols (Cambridge, 2010), p. 1078.

19 XIX, 1–8 and 56–66.

20 Harvey and Paterson, eds, *Tensos*, p. 1088.

21 XXII, 1–10, 36–40, 41–6, 73–88.

22 Linskill, *Raimbaut*, p. 196.

23 See Paolo Squillacioti, 'Raimbaut de Vaqueiras, *Las frevols venson lo plus fort* (BdT 392.21), LT, I, 2008.

24 On authorship see Constanzo Di Girolamo, *I trovatori* (Turin, 1989), pp. 206–10, and BEdT, 392.16a and 392.5a, tradizione manoscritta, ipotesi di attibuzione.

25 I, 16–30.

26 See Federico Saviotti, 'Raimbaut de Vaqueiras', with historical details by Francesca Sanguineti, www.rialto.unina.it, accessed 7 July 2023.

27 Gilda Caïti-Russo, 'Appunti per una lettura "malaspiniana" del contrasto bilingue di Rambaldo di Vaqueiras', in *Atti del convegno di studi 'Poeti e poesia a Genova (e dintorni) nell'età medieval' (Genova, Palazzo Balbi-Cattaneo, 25–26 novembre 2004)*, ed. Margherita Lecco (Alessandria, 2006), pp. 198–204 (p. 199); see her analysis in LT, II (2009), pp. 1–19. See also Furio Brugnolo, *Plurilinguismo e lirica medievale da Raimbaut de Vaqueiras a Dante* (Rome, 1983).

28 Harvey and Paterson, eds, *Tensos*, I, p. 70; Raimbaut's threats to return to the land of Tortona to seek better fortune (V, 37–8) or 'mercy' (VI, 21–2) may well also be jokey references to the fictitious *Genoesa*.

29 See Linda Paterson, 'Insultes, amour et une *trobairitz*: la tenso de Raimbaut de Vaqueiras et Albert Malaspina (PC 15.1)', in *La Voix*

occitane. *Actes du VIIIe Congrès de l'Association Internationale d'Études Occitanes, 12–17 octobre 2005*, ed. Guy Latry, 2 vols (Bordeaux, 2009), vol. I, pp. 227–36.

30 XV, 1–14.

31 Costanzo Di Girolamo, *I trovatori* (Turin, 1989), pp. 210–11.

9 Folquet de Marselha

1 BSC, p. 470.

2 Nicole M. Schulman, *Where Troubadours Were Bishops: The Occitania of Folc of Marseille (1150–1231)* (New York and London, 2001), pp. 43–4.

3 Ibid., pp. 4, 63, 183.

4 Paolo Squillacioti, *Le poesie di Folchetto di Marsiglia* (Pisa, 1999), p. 107 and nn. 162–3.

5 Ibid., pp. 96–111.

6 Ibid., pp. 33–4, revising Stanislav Stronński, *Le troubadour Folquet de Marseille* (Kraków, 1910). Text numbers in this chapter refer to Squillacioti's edition.

7 Schulman, *Where Troubadours Were Bishops*, p. 8.

8 I, 41–7 and 53; VI, 33; Squillacioti, *Poesie*, pp. 35–40; *Dizionario*, p. 191a. With regards to the *Dizionario*, Folquet's address to Alfonso VIII of Castile in XVIII, 46, is no proof of personal contact.

9 Squillacioti, *Poesie*, pp. 93–5.

10 Schulman, *Where Troubadours Were Bishops*, p. 11.

11 Caroline Locher, 'Folquet de Marseille and the Structure of the Canso', *Neophilologus*, LXIV (1980), pp. 192–207; Ugo Sesini, 'Folchetto da Marsiglia, poeta e musicista', *Convivium*, I (1938), pp. 75–84, pp. 82 and 83–4; Squillacioti, *Le poesie*, p. 290.

12 For a transcription of the tune see Hendrik van der Werf, *The Extant Troubadour Melodies: Transcriptions and Essays for Performers and Scholars* (Rochester, NY, 1984), p. 96.

13 Ruth Harvey and Linda Paterson, eds, *The Troubadour Tensos and Partimens: A Critical Edition*, 3 vols (Cambridge, 2010), p. 368.

14 Schulman, *Where Troubadours Were Bishops*, p. 43.

15 Squillacioti, *Le poesie*, pp. 33–4 and 453–7.

16 Linda Paterson, *The World of the Troubadours: Medieval Occitan Society, c. 1100–c. 1300* (Cambridge, 1993), pp. 334–5.

17 Schulman, *Where Troubadours Were Bishops*, p. 77; William A. Sibly and Michael D. Sibly, eds and trans., *The Chronicle of William of Puylaurens: The Albigensian Crusade and Its Aftermath* (Woodbridge, 2003), pp. 24–5.

18 Jonathan Sumption, *The Albigensian Crusade* (London and Boston, MA, 1978), p. 227.
19 Schulman, *Where Troubadours Were Bishops*, p. 45.
20 Ibid., p. 65.
21 William A. Sibly and Michael D. Sibly, eds and trans., *The History of the Albigensian Crusade: Peter of les Vaux-de-Cernay* (Woodbridge, 1998), p. 114.
22 Sibly and Sibly, eds and trans., *William of Puylaurens*, pp. 7, 49, 57, 86, 21–2.
23 Eugène Martin-Chabot, *La Chanson de la croisade albigeoise*, 3 vols (Paris, 1972), 46.2 and 9–12 (see 47.5–15), 68.2–23 and 32–3. All references to the song are from this edition.
24 Ibid., 141.30–36.
25 Ibid., 175.11–44.
26 Ibid., 176.75–8.
27 Gérard Gouiran, 'Drama Queen? Worse: A Jongleur! – or, How to Discredit an Opponent: The Representation of Bishop Fulk of Toulouse, Alias Folquet de Marseille, by the Anonymous Author of the *Song of the Albigensian Crusade*', in Gérard Gouiran, *From Chanson de Geste to Epic Chronicle: Medieval Occitan Poetry of War*, ed. and trans. Linda Paterson (London and New York, 2020), pp. 123–35 (pp. 123–4).
28 Martin-Chabot, *La Chanson*, 145.62–7.
29 Gouiran, 'Drama Queen?', pp. 134–5.
30 Schulman, *Where Troubadours Were Bishops*, p. 176.
31 Stronński, *Folquet de Marseille*, p. 99.

Afterword

1 Miriam Cabré, 'Italian and Catalan Troubadours', in *The Troubadours: An Introduction*, ed. Simon Gaunt and Sarah Kay (Cambridge, 1999), pp. 127–40; Paolo Di Luca and Marco Grimaldi, *L'Italia dei trovatori* (Rome, 2017).
2 Cabré, 'Italian and Catalan Troubadours', p. 138; see also her *Cerverí de Girona and His Poetic Traditions* (London, 1999).
3 Linda Paterson, *The World of the Troubadours: Medieval Occitan Society, c. 1100–c. 1300* (Cambridge, 1993), p. 340, and Roger I. Moore, *The Formation of a Persecuting Society* (Oxford, 1987), p. 51.
4 Linda Paterson, *Singing the Crusades: French and Occitan Lyric Responses to the Crusading Movements, 1137–1336* (Cambridge,

2018), pp. 154–66, 235–44; Eliza Ghil, *L'Age de Parage. Essai sur le poétique et le politique en Occitanie au XIIIe siècle* (New York, 1989).

5 Paterson, *Singing*, Appendix B; Federico S. Annunziata, 'Federico II, l'Italia e le voci del *Midi*', in Paolo Di Luca and Marco Grimaldi, *L'Italia dei trovatori* (Rome, 2017), pp. 1–31.

6 Monica Longobardi, ed., 'I *vers* del trovatore Guiraut Riquier', *Studi mediolatini e volgari*, XXIX (1982–3), pp. 17–163, XXVI, 16.

7 Jean Dunbabin, 'Charles of Anjou: Crusaders and Poets', in *Literature of the Crusades*, ed. Simon T. Parsons and Linda M. Paterson (Cambridge, 2018), pp. 150–57 (p. 151); Stefano Asperti, *Carlo I d'Angió e i trovatori. Componenti "provenzali" e angoine nella tradizione manoscritta della lirica trobadorica* (Ravenna, 1995), pp. 213–14.

8 Paterson, *Singing*, pp. 192–6.

BIBLIOGRAPHY

Annunziata, Francesco S., 'Federico II, l'Italia e le voci del *Midi*', in *L'Italia dei trovatori*, ed. Paolo Di Luca and M. Grimaldi (Rome, 2017), pp. 1–31

Asperti, Stefano, *Il trovatore Raimon Jordan* (Modena, 1990)

—, *Carlo I d'Angió e i trovatori. Componenti 'provenzali' e angoine nella tradizione manoscritta della lirica trobadorica* (Ravenna, 1995)

—, 'Miei-sirventes vueilh far dels reis amdos (BdT 80,25)', *Cultura Neolatina*, LVIII (1998), pp. 165–323

—, 'L'eredità lirica di Bertran de Born', *Cultura Neolatina*, LXIV (2004), pp. 475–525

—, 'Don Johanz la sap: musicisti e lirica romanza in Lombardia nel Trecento', in *Studi di filologia romanza offerti a Valeria Bertolucci Pizzorusso*, ed. Pietro G. Beltrami et al., 2 vols (Pisa, 2006), vol. I, pp. 67–90

Aurell, Martin, '*Fin'amors*, féodalité et *wadd* dans la lyrique des troubadours', in *L'éspace lyrique méditerranéen au Moyen Age: nouvelles approches. Actes du colloque de l'Université de Nantes, 25–27 mars 2004*, ed. Dominique Billy, François Clément and Annie Combes (Toulouse, 2006)

—, 'Guillaume IX et l'Islam', in *Guilhem de Peitieus, duc d'Aquitaine, prince du trobar. Trobadas tenues à Bordeaux (Lormont) les 20–21 septembre 2013 et à Poitiers les 12–13 septembre 2014* (Ventadour, 2015), pp. 69–126

Bampa, Alessandro, 'La maturité du corpus du "premier troubadour"', in TBP, pp. 205–17

Banniard, Michel, 'Guillaume et le latin de son temps: quelques arrière-plans langagiers', in TBP, pp. 275–86

Barbieri, Luca, 'A *mon Ynsombart part Troia*. Une polémique anti-courtoise dans le dialoque entre trouvères et troubadours', *Medioevo Romanzo*, XXXVII (2013), pp. 264–95

—, 'Le canzoni di crociata e il canone lirico oitanico', *Medioevi*, I (2015), pp. 45–74

Bec, Pierre, *Arnaut Daniel. 'Fin' amor' et folie du verbe* (Paris, 2012)
—, *Burlesque et obscénité chez les troubadours: pour une approche du contre-texte médiéval* (Paris, 1984)
—, *Chants d'amour des femmes troubadours* (Paris, 1995)
—, *Le comte de Poitiers, premier troubadour. A l'aube d'un verbe et d'une érotique* (Montpellier, 2010)
—, 'Jaufre Rudel et les poètes romantiques allemands', in TB, pp. 21–34
Beggiato, Fabrizio, *Il trovatore Bernart Marti* (Modena, 1984)
Billy, Dominique, *L'architecture lyrique médiévale. Analyse métrique et modélisation des structures interstrophiques dans la poésie lyrique des troubadours et des trouvères* (Montpellier, 1989)
—, 'L'art poétique d'Arnaut Daniel', in TR, pp. 107–31
Blamires, Alcuin, Karen Pratt and C. William Marx, eds, *Woman Defamed and Woman Defended: An Anthology of Medieval Texts* (Oxford, 1992)
Bond, Gerald A., *The Poetry of William VII, Count of Poitiers, IX Duke of Aquitaine* (New York and London, 1982)
Boutoulle, Frédéric, 'L'appel du large. Jaufre Rudel et les autres seigneurs de Blaye aux XIe, XIIe et XIIIe siècles', in TB, pp. 81–101
Bruckner, Matilda, Laurie Shepard and Sarah White, *Songs of the Women Troubadours* (New York and London, 1995)
Brugnolo, Furio, *Plurilinguismo e lirica medievale da Raimbaut de Vaqueiras a Dante* (Rome, 1983)
Brundage, James A., *Law, Sex, and Christian Society in Medieval Europe* (Chicago, 1987)
Burgwinkle, William E., 'Raimbaut de Vaqueiras et les rites de l'identité', in *Scène, évolution, sort de la langue et de la littérature d'oc. Actes du Septième Congrès International d'Études Occitanes, Reggio Calabria – Messina, 7–13 juillet 2002*, ed. Rossana Castano, Saverio Guida and Fortunata Latella, 2 vols (Rome, 2003), vol. I, pp. 157–65
Cabré, Miriam, *Cerverí de Girona and His Poetic Traditions* (London, 1999)
—, 'Italian and Catalan Troubadours', in *The Troubadours: An Introduction*, ed. Simon Gaunt and Sarah Kay (Cambridge, 1999), pp. 127–40
Caïti-Russo, Gilda, *Les troubadours à la cour des Malaspina* (Montpellier, 2005)
—, 'Appunti per una lettura "malaspiniana" del contrasto bilingue di Rambaldo di Vaqueiras', in *Atti del convegno di studi 'Poeti e poesia a Genova (e dintorni) nell'età medievale' (Genova, Palazzo*

Balbi-Cattaneo, 25–26 novembre 2004), ed. Margherita Lecco (Alessandria, 2006), pp. 198–204

Carapezza, Francesco, 'Canzoni "date in moglie" a sirventesi nella *vida II* di Bertran de Born', CN, 68 (2008), pp. 315–33

—, 'Le côté musical d'Arnaut Daniel: remarques sur les structures strophiques de ses chansons', in TR, pp. 55–75

—, 'Ecouter Bernart de Ventadorn. Lecture de quatre *unica* musicaux: BdT 70.42 (X), 24 (W), 17 (G) et 25 (R)', in TD, pp. 3–12

—, 'Le melodie perdute di Guglielmo IX', in '*Que ben devetz conoisser la plus fina*'. *Per Margherita Spampinato*, ed. M. Pagano (Rome, 2018)

—, 'La dimensione musicale dei trovatori', LT, XIII (2020), pp. 127–63

Chaillou-Amadieu, Christelle, 'Les exécutions musicales de Guillaume d'Aquitaine: entre réécriture et reconstitution', in TBP, pp. 251–64

Chiarini, Giorgio, *Il canzoniere di Jaufre Rudel* (L'Aquila, 1985)

Cuesta, Ismael Fernández de la, and Robert Lafont, *Las Cançons dels trobadors* (Toulouse, 1979)

Dante, *The Divine Comedy of Dante Alighieri*, ed. and trans. Robert M. Durling, 3 vols (Oxford, 2003)

—, *De vulgari eloquentia*, ed. Steven Botterill (Cambridge, 2009)

Denomy, Alexander J., '*Fin'amors*: The Pure Love of the Troubadours: Its Amorality and Possible Source', *Medieval Studies*, VII (1945), pp. 139–207

Di Girolamo, Costanzo, *I trovatori* (Turin, 1989)

—, ed., Guglielmo di Poitiers, 'Molt jauzens mi prenc an amar' (BdT 183.8), in LT, VII (2014), pp. 1–32

Di Luca, Paolo, '*Sirventesca*: le sirventes parodié', *Revue des langues romanes*, CXII (2008), pp. 405–34

—, 'Blacasset, *Se·l mals d'amor m'auzi ni m'es noisens* (BdT 96.10a), Pujol, *Dieus es amors e verais salvamens* (BdT 386.2), Alaisina ~ Carenza, *Na Carenza al bel cors avenenç* (BdT 12.1 = 108.1)', in LT, IV (2011)

—, and M. Grimaldi, *L'Italia dei trovatori* (Rome, 2017)

Dronke, Peter, 'The Song of Songs and Medieval Love-Lyric', in *The Bible and Medieval Culture*, ed. Willem Lourdaux and Daniël Verhelst (Leuven, 1979), pp. 237–62

—, *Women Writers of the Middle Ages: A Critical Study of Texts from Perpetua (d. 203) to Marguerite Porete (d. 1310)* (Cambridge, 1984)

Duby, Georges, *The Knight, the Lady and the Priest: The Making of Modern Marriage in Medieval France* (Harmondsworth, 1985)

Dunbabin, Jean, 'Charles of Anjou: Crusaders and Poets', in *Literature of the Crusades*, ed. Simon Thomas Parsons and Linda M. Paterson (Cambridge, 2018), pp. 150–57

Eusebi, Mario, *Arnaut Daniel: 'L'aur'amara* (Milan, 1984)

Faral, Edmond, *Les jongleurs en France au moyen âge* (Paris, 1971)

Ferrari, Anna, 'Bernart de Ventadorn ou l'apogée de la courtoisie', in TD, pp. 77–92

Formisano, Luciano, 'Prospettive di ricerca sui canzonieri d'autore nella lira d'oïl', in *La filologia romanza e i codici. Atti del convegno, Messina, Università degli studi, Facoltà di lettere e filosofia, 19–22 decembre 1991*, ed. Saverio Guida and Fortunata Latella, Messina (1994), I, pp. 131–52

Francesco Petrarca, *Trionfi, rime estravaganti, codice degli abbozzi*, ed. Vinicio Pacca and Laura Paolino (Milan, 1996)

Frank, István, *Répertoire métrique de la poésie des troubadours*, 2 vols (Paris, 1953–7)

Fratta, Aniello, *Peire d'Alvernhe, Poesie* (Rome, 1996)

Gaunt, Simon, Ruth Harvey and Linda Paterson, *Marcabru: A Critical Edition* (Cambridge, 2000)

Gaunt, Simon, and Sarah Kay, ed., *The Troubadours: An Introduction* (Cambridge, 1999)

Ghil, Eliza, *L'Age de Parage. Essai sur le poétique et le politique en Occitanie au XIIIe siècle* (New York, 1989)

Gillingham, John, *Richard Coeur de Lion* (Paris, 1996)

Goddard, Richard, *The Early Troubadours and the Latin Tradition* (Maastricht, 2017)

Goldin, Frederick, *The Mirror of Narcissus in the Courtly Love Lyric* (Ithaca, NY, 1968)

Gouiran, Gérard, 'Bertran de Born, poète de l'amour', in *Chrétien de Troyes and the Troubadours: Essays in Memory of the late L. Topsfield*, ed. Peter Noble and Linda Paterson (Cambridge, 1984), pp. 52–6

—, *L'amour et la guerre. L'oeuvre de Bertran de Born*, 2 vols (Aix-en-Provence, 1985)

—, 'Drama Queen? Worse: A Jongleur! – or, How to Discredit an Opponent: The Representation of Bishop Fulk of Toulouse, Alias Folquet de Marseille, by the Anonymous Author of the *Song of the Albigensian Crusade*', in Gérard Gouiran, *From Chanson de Geste to Epic Chronicle: Medieval Occitan Poetry of War*, ed. and trans. Linda Paterson (London and New York, 2020), pp. 123–35

Gruber, Jörn, *Die Dialektik der Trobar* (Tübingen, 1983)

Guida, Saverio, 'Aspetti sociologici delle biografie provenzali', in *Atti del Secondo Congresso della Association Inernationale d'Études Occitanes, Torino, 31 agosto–5 settembre 1987*, 2 vols (Turin, 1993)

—, 'Il quinto bersaglio di Peire d'Alvernhe nella satira *Chantarai d'aquestz trobador*', *Revista di leteratura medieval*, XXXI (2019), pp. 97–140

Haines, John, *Medieval Song in Romance Languages* (Cambridge, 2010)

Haines, John, J. Butt, and Laurence Dreyfus, *Eight Centuries of Troubadours and Trouvères: The Changing Identity of Medieval Music* (Cambridge, 2004)

Harvey, Ruth, 'The Troubadour Marcabru and His Public', *Reading Medieval Studies*, XIV (1988), pp. 47–76

—, *The Troubadour Marcabru and Love* (London, 1989)

—, 'The Professional Status of the Early Troubadours', in *Medieval Occitan Language and Literature: Sixth Annual Conference* (Cambridge, 1991)

—, 'The Wives of the "First Troubadour", Duke William IX of Aquitaine', *Journal of Medieval History*, XIX (1993), pp. 307–25

—, 'Courtly Culture in Medieval Occitania', in *The Troubadours: An Introduction*, ed. Simon Gaunt and Sarah Kay (Cambridge, 1999)

—, review of Saverio Guida and Gerardo Larghi, *Dizionario biografici dei trovatori* (Modena, 2013) in *Tenso*, XXXII (2017), pp. 41–6

Harvey, Ruth, and Linda Paterson, *The Troubadour Tensos and Partimens: A Critical Edition*, 3 vols (Cambridge, 2010)

Kay, Sarah, 'Love in a Mirror: An Aspect of the Imagery of Bernart de Ventadorn', *Medium Aevum*, LII (1983), pp. 272–85

—, 'Derivation, Derived Rhyme, and the Trobairitz', in *The Voice of the Trobairitz: Perspectives on the Women Troubadours*, ed. William D. Paden (Philadelphia, PA, 1989), pp. 157–82

—, *Subjectivity in Troubadour Poetry* (Cambridge, 1990)

Lachin, Giosué, *Il trovatore Elias Cairel* (Modena, 2004)

Laurent, Sébastien-Abel, 'Le troubadour Jaufre Rudel de Blaye: un proche des ducs d'Aquitaine devenu rebelle?', in *Fidélités et dissidences. Actes du XIIe congrès de l'Association internationale des Études occitanes, Albi, 10–15 juillet 2017*, ed. Jean-François Courouau and David Fabié (Toulouse, 2020), pp. 499–508

Lavaud, René, and René Nelli, *Les troubadours. Jaufre, Flamenca, Barlaam et Josaphat* (Paris, 1969)

Lazar, Moshé, *Bernard de Ventadour, troubadour du XIIe siècle: chansons d'amour* (Paris, 1966)

Lazzerini, Lucia, '*Chaitius clamatz* clé d'une chanson de croisade?', in TB, pp. 186–96
—, *Les troubadours et la sagesse* (Ventadour, 2013)
—, 'Le chant de Bernart de Ventadorn entre motifs folkloriques et postérité poético-théologique', in TD, pp. 45–63
Linskill, Joseph, *The Poems of the Troubadour Raimbaut de Vaqueiras* (The Hague, 1964)
Livingstone, Amy, '"Daughter of Fulk, Glory of Brittany": Countess Ermengarde of Brittany (*c.* 1070–1147)', *Anglo-Norman Studies*, XL (2018), pp. 165–78
Locher, Caroline, 'Folquet de Marseille and the Structure of the Canso', *Neophilologus*, LXIV (1980), pp. 192–207
Longobardi, Monica, 'I vers del trovatore Guiraut Riquier', *Studi mediolatini e volgari*, XXIX (1982–3), pp. 17–163
Lug, Robert, 'Jaufre Rudel rajeuni', in TB, pp. 57–79
Makin, Peter, *Provence and Pound* (Berkeley, CA, 1978)
Martin-Chabot, Eugène, *La Chanson de la croisade albigeoise*, 3 vols (Paris, 1972)
Martindale, Jane, '*Cavalaria et Orgueill*: Duke William IX of Aquitaine and the Historian', in *Status, Authority and Regional Power: Aquitaine and France, 9th to 12th Centuries* (Aldershot, 1997)
Matter, E. Ann, *The Voice of My Beloved: The Song of Songs in Western Medieval Christianity* (Philadelphia, PA, 2010)
Melani, Sylvio, 'l cammino della croce e gli artigli della lussuria: ipotesi sulle "perdute" *cantilenae* composte da Guglielmo IX in occasione della sua crociata', in *Le letterature romanze del Medioevo: testi, storia, intersezioni. Atti del V Convegno Nazionale della SIFR*, ed. Antonio Pioletti (Rome, 2000), pp. 281–93
Meliga, Walter, 'Le *sen* de Bertran de Born', in TH, pp. 21–32
—, 'Brève récapitulation de l'amor de lonh', in TB, pp. 172–8
—, 'Conclusion de la *Trobada*', in TR, pp. 145–51
—, 'La postérité du comte de Poitiers', in TBP, pp. 343–52
Milonia, Stefano, *Rima e melodia nell'arte allusiva dei trovatori* (Rome, 2016)
Moore, Robert I., *The Formation of a Persecuting Society* (Oxford, 1987)
Mynors, Roger A. B., Rodney M. Thomson and Michael Winterbottom, ed. and trans., *Gesta regum Anglorum: The History of the English Kings* (Oxford, 1998)
Nelli, René, *L'Erotique des troubadours* (Toulouse, 1963)
Nichols, Stephen G., *The Songs of Bernart de Ventadorn* (Chapel Hill, NC, 1962)

Noble, Peter, and Linda Paterson, *Chrétien de Troyes and the Troubadours: Essays in Memory of the Late L. Topsfield* (Cambridge, 1984)

Noto, Giuseppe, *Il giullare e il trovatore nelle liriche e nelle 'biografie' provenzali* (Alessandria, 1998)

Orderic Vitalis, *The Ecclesiastical History*, ed. Marjorie Chibnall, 5 vols (Oxford, 1975)

Paden, William D., Tilda Sankovitch and Patricia H. Stäblein, *The Poems of the Troubadour Bertran de Born* (Berkeley, CA, and London, 1986)

—, *The Voice of the Trobairitz: Perspectives on the Women Troubadours* (Philadelphia, PA, 1989)

Parsons, Simon Thomas, and Linda M. Paterson, *Literature of the Crusades* (Cambridge, 2018)

Pasero, Nicolo, *Guglielmo IX d'Aquitania, Poesie* (Modena, 1973)

Paterson, Linda, *Troubadours and Eloquence* (Oxford, 1975)

—, *The World of the Troubadours: Medieval Occitan Society, c. 1100–c. 1300* (Cambridge, 1993)

—, '*Fin'amor* and the Development of the Courtly *Canso*', in *The Troubadours: An Introduction*, ed. Simon Gaunt and Sarah Kay (Cambridge, 1999), pp. 28–31

—, 'Les *tensons* et *partimens*', in *Les Troubadours*, ed. Max Rouquette and Tommaso Landolfi, *Europe*, LXXXVI (June–July 2008), pp. 102–14

—, 'Insultes, amour et une *trobairitz*: la tenso de Raimbaut de Vaqueiras et Albert Malaspina (PC 15.1)', in *La Voix occitane. Actes du VIIIe Congrès de l'Association Internationale d'Études Occitanes, 12–17 octobre 2005*, ed. Guy Latry, 2 vols (Bordeaux, 2009), vol. I, pp. 227–36

—, 'Greeks and Latins at the Time of the Fourth Crusade: Patriarch John X Kamateros and a Troubadour *Tenso*', in *Languages of Love and Hate: Conflict, Communication, and Identity in the Medieval Mediterranean*, ed. Sarah Lambert and Helen Nicholson (Turnhout, 2012), pp. 119–39

—, 'Anonymous (Nompar de Caumont?), *Finament* (BdT 461.122)', in LT (2014)

—, *Singing the Crusades: French and Occitan Lyric Responses to the Crusading Movements, 1137–1336* (Cambridge, 2018)

—, 'Centres et périphéries: la civilisation littéraire occitane et son espacement dans le temps et les régions', p. 88, in press

Pattison, Walter T., *The Life and Works of the Troubadour Raimbaut d'Orange* (Minneapolis, MN, 1952)

Pauvert, Dominique, with Christine Escarmant, 'Arnaut Daniel, maître du *cornar ric*', in TR, pp. 39–53

Pécout, Thierry, *L'invention de la Provence: Raymond Bérenger v* (Paris, 2004)

Perugi, Maurizio, 'Arnaut Daniel, un troubadour de renommée internationale', in TR, pp. 29–38

Pollina, Vincent, 'Les mélodies du troubadour Marcabru: questions de style et de genre', in *Atti del Secondo Congresso Internazionale delle 'Association Internationale d'Études Occitanes'*, ed. Giuliano Gasca Queirazza, 2 vols (Turin, 1993), vol. I, pp. 289–306

Rieger, Angelica, '"Ins e.l cor port, dona, vostre faisso". Image et imaginaire de la femme à travers l'enluminure dans les chansonniers des troubadours', *Cahiers de Civilisation Médiévale*, XXVII (1885), pp. 385–415

—, *Trobairitz. Der Beitrag der Frau in der altokzitanischen höfischen Lyrik* (Tübingen, 1991)

Riquer, Martín de, *Los Trovadores*, 3 vols (Barcelona, 1975)

Rodríguez Winiarski, M. Victoria, 'The *Trobairitz*', www.trob-eu.net, accessed 7 July 2023

Rosenberg, Samuel, Margaret Switten and Gérard Le Vot, *Songs of the Troubadours and Trouvères: An Anthology of Poems and Melodies* (New York and London, 1998)

Rosenstein, Roy, 'Jaufre Rudel au pluriel: les Jaufre Rudel de Blaya et d'ailleurs', in TB, pp. 103–14

—, 'Arnaut Daniel parle-t-il portugais?', in TR, pp. 93–106

Roubaud, Jacques, *Les Troubadours. Anthologie bilingue* (Paris, 1980)

—, 'L'Etrange destin de la *canson* "Lo ferm voler" d'Arnaut Daniel', in TR, pp. 133–43

Sansone, Giuseppe E., *Testi didattico-cortese di Provenza* (Bari, 1977)

Saviotti, Federico, 'Il viaggio del poeta e il viaggio del testo: per un approccio geografico a Raimbaut de Vaqueiras e alla sua tradizione manoscritta', *Moderna*, x (2008), Fascicle 2, pp. 43–59

—, 'Federico II, l'Italia e le voci del *Midi*', in Paolo Di Luca and Marco Grimaldi, *L'Italia dei trovatori* (Rome, 2017), pp. 1–31

—, '*Senhals* et pseudonymes, entre Raimon de Cornet et Raimbaut de Vaqueiras', in *Actes du XXVIIe Congrès international de linguistique et de philologie romanes (Nancy, 15–20 juillet 2013). Section 14: Littératures médiévales*, *Nancy*, ed. Isabel de Riquer, Dominique Billy and G. Palumbo (Nancy, 2017), pp. 195–204

Schulman, Nicole M., *Where Troubadours Were Bishops: The Occitania of Folc of Marseille (1150–1231)* (New York and London, 2001)

Sesini, Ugo, 'Folchetto da Marsiglia, poeta e musicista', *Convivium*, I (1938), pp. 75–84

Sharman, Ruth V., *The Cansos and Sirventes of the Troubadour Giraut de Borneil* (Cambridge, 1989)

Sibly, William A., and Michael D. Sibly, ed. and trans., *The History of the Albigensian Crusade: Peter of les Vaux-de-Cernay* (Woodbridge, 1998)

—, *The Chronicle of William of Puylaurens: The Albigensian Crusade and Its Aftermath* (Woodbridge, 2003)

Squillacioti, Paolo, *Le poesie di Folchetto di Marsiglia* (Pisa, 1999)

Stewart, Stanley, *The Enclosed Garden: The Tradition and the Image in Seventeenth-Century Poetry* (Madison, WI, 1966)

Stronński, Stanislaw, *Le troubadour Folquet de Marseille* (Kraków, 1910)

Sumption, Jonathan, *The Albigensian Crusade* (London and Boston, MA, 1978)

Switten, Margaret, *The Cansos of Raimon de Miraval: A Study of the Poems and Melodies* (Cambridge, MA, 1985)

—, 'Music and Versification. Fetz Marcabrus los mots e.l so', in *The Troubadours: An Introduction*, ed. Simon Gaunt and Sarah Kay (Cambridge, 1999), pp. 141–63

Thuillat, Jean-Pierre, *Bertran de Born. Histoire et légende* (Périgueux, 2009)

Toja, Gianluigi, *Arnaut Daniel, canzoni* (Florence, 1960)

Topsfield, Leslie, *Troubadours and Love* (Cambridge, 1975)

Tortoreto, Valeria, *Il trovatore Cercamon* (Modena, 1981)

Waddell, Helen, *The Wandering Scholars* (London and Toronto, 1927, repr. 1942)

—, *Medieval Latin Lyrics* (Harmondsworth, 1929, repr. 1962)

Weir, Anthony, and James Jerman, *Images of Lust: Sexual Carvings on Medieval Churches* (London, 1986)

Werf, Hendrik van der, *The Extant Troubadour Melodies: Transcriptions and Essays for Performers and Scholars* (Rochester, NY, 1984)

Zufferey, François, 'Nouvelle approche de l'amour de loin', *Cultura Neolatina*, LXIX (2009), pp. 7–58

—, 'Toward a Delimitation of the Trobairitz Corpus', in *The Voice of the Trobairitz: Perspectives on the Women Troubadours*, ed. William D. Paden (Philadelphia, PA, 1989), pp. 31–43

ACKNOWLEDGEMENTS

My heartfelt thanks go to Ruth Harvey for unstintingly making herself available throughout the writing of this book, offering me information and wise advice and steering me away from errors. Any remaining are my own, of course. My warm gratitude also goes to Francesco Carapezza for his advice on music, to Mike Paterson for his customary patience, technical and moral support and his mathematical contribution to Chapter Six, and to Michael Leaman and Alex Ciobanu of Reaktion Books, who have been generous with their time and guidance on the book's preparation. Richard Goddard kindly gave me permission to quote freely from his book *The Early Troubadours and the Latin Tradition*, and Sarah Kay from her article 'Love in a Mirror: An Aspect of the Imagery of Bernart de Ventadorn' (*Medium Aevum*, LII (1983), pp. 272–85).

PHOTO ACKNOWLEDGEMENTS

The author and publishers wish to express their thanks to the sources listed below for illustrative material and/or permission to reproduce it. Some locations of artworks are also given below, in the interest of brevity:

Arxiu de la Corona d'Aragó, Barcelona: p. 14 (Canc. Reg. 01, fol. 1r); Biblioteca da Ajuda, Lisbon: p. 10 (fol. 55v); Biblioteca Nazionale Ambrosiana, Milan: p. 145 (MS R 71 sup, fol. 73r); Bibliothèque de l'Arsenal, Paris: p. 169 (MS 5090 réserve, fol. 205r); Bibliothèque nationale de France, Paris: pp. 8 (MS Latin 1118, fol. 112v), 11 (MS Français 12473, fol. 4r), 20 (MS Français 12473, fol. 79r), 21 (MS Français 12473, fol. 121r), 22 (MS Français 854, fol. 49r), 28 (MS Français 22543, fol. 107r), 36 (MS Français 854, fol. 142v), 52 (MS Français 12473, fol. 107v), 56 (MS Français 854, fol. 121v), 60 (MS Français 20050, fol. 81v), 66 (MS Français 12473, fol. 102r), 71 (MS Français 22495, fol. 154v), 86 (MS Français 12473, fol. 15v), 95 (MS Français 22543, fol. 56v), 110 (MS Français 12473, fol. 125v), 112 (*top*; MS Français 854, fol. 125r), 112 (*bottom*; MS Français 854, fol. 141r), 130 (MS Français 12473, fol. 50r), 148 (MS Français 12473, fol. 160r), 156 (MS Français 2754, fol. 198r), 168 (MS Français 854, fol. 75v), 188 (MS Français 12474, fol. 25r), 202 (MS Français 12473, fol. 46r); from Louis Blancard, *Iconographie des sceaux et bulles conservés dans la partie antérieure à 1790 . . .* (Marseille and Paris, 1860), photo Princeton University Library, NJ: p. 122; British Library, London: pp. 194–5 (Royal MS 16 G VI, fol. 374v); Fiske Dante Collection, Division of Rare and Manuscript Collections, Cornell University Library, Ithaca, NY: p. 157; Flickr: pp. 41 (photo Tony Hisgett/ahisgett, CC BY 2.0), 72 (photo gongoozlr, CC BY-SA 2.0), 111 (photo Patrick/Morio60, CC BY-SA 2.0), 161 (photo gongoozlr, CC BY-SA 2.0); map Linda M. Paterson: p. 12; diagrams Mike Paterson: pp. 142, 143; Real Biblioteca del Monasterio de San Lorenzo de El Escorial, courtesy Patrimonio Nacional: p. 24 (MS B-I-2, fol. 29r); Universitätsbibliothek Heidelberg: p. 15 (Cod. Pal. germ. 848, fol. 181v); Wikimedia Commons: p. 186 (photo Didier Devèze/Ddeveze, CC BY-SA 4.0).

INDEX

Page numbers in *italics* refer to illustrations